Making Your Own Wine

What it's Really Like to Start, Run and Profitably
Sell a Vineyard and Winery

Peter Svans

ISBN: 1469900070X
ISBN-13: 978-1469900704

DEDICATION

This is for every wine lover who's sat with a glass in front of them and dreamt about what it's like to make your own wine in your own winery with grapes from your own vineyard.

Always follow your dreams...

And to Peter and Yolanda Kozik and their wonderful children: James, Amanda and David. You only ever get to see a person's true colours when the chips are down and I can say the Koziks are the finest people in my life.

CONTENTS

ACKNOWLEDGMENTS

You can't do something like this alone.
This is for everyone who bought our wines, came to our functions, read our newsletters and shared our dreams.

1 INTRODUCTION

I love my wines and always dreamt about making my own wines from grapes grown in my own vineyard.

Peter, Yolanda and I started making wines in small batches in the backyard. We'd pick a few hundred kilograms of grapes and turn the cabana into a suburban winery. At times I'm sure the neighbourhood was drunk just from the fumes.

When we'd finished processing I'd run up and down the street on garbage night stuffing the bins with leftover stalks, pressings or whatever we had to get rid of.

And then the 'commercial' wine making bug bit and bit hard.

Like all good plans hatched over a few bottles of red we decided to ignore reality and chase the dream to make our own wines on a bigger scale.

In the late 1980s we started looking for a vacant block of land where we'd plant our own vines, put up the cellar door and survey our world supping a glass of the best wines ever made: ours.

We looked at many, many vacant blocks and brought in consultants to assess our choices as vacant land was all that fitted our budget. But after 3 years we were still landless and stuck in our day jobs.

Purely by chance Peter K spotted a small "for auction" advert in the corner of The Weekly Times. It was way out of our price range but Peter K and Yolanda drove out to check it out.

It was perfect.

It was less than 100km from Melbourne, it was off the main road to one of Australia's biggest tourist attractions, there were stunning views down over the water, some vines were in the ground, it had basic winemaking/vineyard equipment and there was a huge sandstone house complete with kangaroos in the backyard mornings and evenings.

We ummmed and ahhhhed for a few hours and called back to put in a bid before the auction. I hadn't seen the place as I was working in Sydney over 1,000km away. But we'd seen so many blocks of land that we knew what we wanted and we knew what we didn't want. To our surprise the owner took our bid and it was ours.

We moved in on New Year's Eve 1992 and our adventures began.

Since that time we've made and sold a helluva lot of wines and had hundreds of thousands of people through the cellar door. And every time I shared our story I got pretty much the same reply:

Wow, we've always wanted to own a winery

I've lost count of how many times I got that reply.

After 18 years on the land we sold the winery in 2010 and this is our story of what it's really like to own a winery.

It's not a textbook, it's not a finance manual and it's not a step-by-step how-to manual. And it's not laid out in date order or order of importance or any other order you can think of.

It's what we did and how we did it and the highs and lows we lived through.

Enjoy the read and always follow your dreams because life is too short to miss out what you really want to do.

2 LIFE AT THE CELLAR DOOR

Tourist Buses

The overseas tourism market was huge for us. Or to say this more accurately, we made it a huge part of our business.

We were not far off the main road linking Melbourne and the Penguin Parade at Phillip Island. The Penguin Parade is the 3rd most visited tourist attraction in Australia. The Opera House takes number 1 spot while the Great Barrie Reef splashes into spot number 2. The winery was about two thirds of the way on the trip out there so it was an ideal place for tour groups to stop in. We decided to go and get the tourism bus market and kept at it until we got them.

The strategy was very simple. We had an outstanding location with breathtaking views, plenty of sweet wines and friendly people behind the bar. There was easy turning space for even the largest coaches and we had clean toilets. Sure, there were other things the tour operators looked for and we made sure we 'ticked the box' in all of them.

I drafted a brochure saying why a tour group should 'break the drive' to Phillip Island and stop at the winery. The more of them I handed out, the more coaches and tour companies did just that. They broke up the drive with another super destination for their customers.

By handing them out, I mean handing them straight to the tour operators. I'd go down to the Penguin Parade and walk from bus to bus, talking to each driver and operator. I'd find the buses when they stopped at the key tourist spots around Melbourne and hand out my brochure. It didn't take long before they all knew me and it took even less time for them to stop in. The first version now seems so quaint and basic, but it worked. It worked damn well.

In the early days we'd take each group down to the vines and give them our 'vineyard' talk. And they thought it was great, people loved this talk even though it was so simple. If you woke me at 2:30am and asked for the vineyard talk, I'd deliver it word-perfect every time. After you've done something a thousand times it tends to stick to you and this did. You'd vary it a little and you'd change the lead-in depending on the season but it was pretty much the same talk.

And here's the talk;

Please don't touch the grapes. During flowering you'll damage the flowers or at other times of the years they're quite fragile or recently sprayed.

These are all cabernet sauvignon vines and they're about 26 years old.

The vine starts to come to life in spring, around the end of September. By mid October there'll be some leaves on the vines and the shoots will be starting to form. Flowering starts about the end of November which is very late for Australia.

When a wine grape is fully grown, it'll be about the size of the top of your little finger. The entire bunch will be about the size of the palm of your hand. When they're ripe, they're sickly sweet. It's not like a table grape where you could eat the entire bunch, you'd be sick if you ate an entire bunch of wine grapes as they're just sugar and water and sickly sweet.

Around the end of January these grapes will start to get a bit of colour in them and this means they're starting to get a bit of sugar in them as well. This is when the birds think this place is a supermarket. As you saw on the way up, there's bush over the other side of the road, there's bush behind us and there's bush all around us. The only way we can protect the crop is to net everything - otherwise there'd be nothing left after just one day. There are kilometres and kilometres of nets that go over the vines.

We'll be harvesting the grapes anywhere from March through to May. The early varieties, the pinot and the chardonnays will come off first and the shiraz and cabernet will always come off last. This is a very late ripening area. The warmer parts of Australia will have harvested by the end of January or February. The long, slow ripening period during autumn gives us the fantastic fruit flavours in the wine. It's like growing a lettuce quickly. The flavour's not the same in a quick grown lettuce as in a slow and steady matured lettuce. We're after the best possible quality fruit we can get.

We harvest the red grapes by machine and the white's by hand. The harvester sits over the top of the row and physically beats the grapes off the stalks. You have big fibreglass rods spaced like fingers that bash the grapes off the stalks and pick them up underneath. This is a lot quicker, cleaner, safer and better quality crop than having forty or fifty people wondering around outside with the cutters and heat and snakes. We can have two people running the harvester and pick a few acres in an afternoon. The grapes are into the winery a lot quicker than having to stack them in boxes and then wait for them to be picked up.

We'll pick around 2 to 3 tons of fruit from one acre of vines. We'll get around 600 litres of wine from one ton of grapes which gives us around 800 bottles.

Once the fruit is picked the leaves will start to fall off the vines at the beginning of winter. Once all the leaves are gone, we'll start pruning. We'll cut all the new canes off and leave just one cane/cordon on the wire. Then come spring, which is late September, the vines will start growing again. So we get one crop per year.

We irrigate the vines by the drippers you see on the black pipe. A sprinkler irrigation system will let the vine form shallow roots near the surface of the earth. A dripper system forces the vines roots down deep into the, up to several metres deep, and this means they can handle a drought better than a shallow rooted vine.

A vine is like a stone fruit or walnut. They need to see a 'cold snap' during the winter so the plant knows it's had its dormant cycle. If there's no cold snap, you'll get an uneven budburst and patchy fruit set. We're doing everything we can to get the best possible quality fruit and an even budburst is crucial to the fruit quality.

Down here we are a very cold climate and it takes a fair while to get established. We do a lot of the work by machine so the ground has to be pretty level. It takes us one year to prepare the soil, to rip the vine row and level it. From the time we plant the vine, it takes 5 years to get the first commercial crop off the vines. After that, it's about two years to get your first bottle from those grapes. So it's about eight years from the time you start with bare grass to your first bottle out the other end. It's not a get rich quick scheme.

The oldest vines we have are 25 years old. The oldest in Australia is 135 years in South Australia and the oldest worldwide is about 400 years out of Switzerland.

Everything we do with the vines is to get the best possible quality fruit. If you've got lousy quality fruit and the worlds best winemaker with the worlds best winemaking equipment, you'll still get a lousy quality wine. If you have the fantastic quality fruit and an average winemaker, you'll still end up with a very, very good wine.

That's about all. Are there any questions?

Later on we upgraded the brochure and had it translated into Traditional Chinese, Modern Chinese and Thai. It was so very simple, but it worked. It worked as it gave people enough information to be comfortable to stop in and see what we were doing. Once they were here, it was up to us to sell them something.

The greatest kick I ever got from this brochure was a carload of folks from mainland China stopping by. They'd found my brochure on the web before they left China and they made a point of stopping in.

I still get a buzz thinking about this. How simple words from country Australia reach someone half way around the world and get them to stop in, that just seems awesome to me. I no longer have the stats on how many times it's been viewed and downloaded, but I know I've printed many thousands so the downloads must be phenomenal.

A lot of our success came from just promoting the buggery out of the place until we got the business. That's it, it was that simple.

Never give in, never give in, never give in.

I'm not the world's greatest copywriter or advertising guru by any stretch of the imagination. But it's amazing what you can get done with some simple books and other stuff. A simple brochure with pretty pictures is nice but not really all that effective. A simple brochure with the right words, offering great value to the customer and then getting that brochure out to 1,000 key targeted people all of a sudden is hugely effective.

And the bills piling up always give you a pretty good incentive to go get 'em.

We set our policy of not offering cash kickbacks and this cost us only one, one single little tour group, over all the years. They were the only group who wanted cash. What we did do to encourage the guides and drivers was to hand out a 'coffee card'. For every dozen bottles their tour group bought, they got a free bottle.

This worked on many levels and it took us a while to figure out why it worked so well and here's what we worked out.

The drivers and guides regularly swapped employers. The Penguin Parade was a key tourist destination around Melbourne so all the guides knew the route and the routine. And just because they were with some other employer this week, that was no reason for them not to stop by their favourite winery. It made them look good to their boss as it was a new no-cost attraction and we made sure to make them look good in front of their customers.

We had lots of loyal fans coming back year after year. They'd stop by in the middle of winter and they'd stop by when summer was melting the pavements.

Some days we'd have over 400 people streaming through the place while other days were pretty quiet.

If a view can ever get 'used up' by having too many photos taken then we must've been close to it.

The busy days left you drained.

Until you've worked in hospitality you have no idea of the mental exhaustion of dealing with hundreds of people. The noise, the demands, you have to keep smiling, you're running around packing bottles, making sure there's toilet paper in the toilets, keeping the eyes in the back of your head open, getting a coffee for my regular drivers and guides and every other thing to keep it all humming. There were days when we'd lock up and limp down to the house and have trouble forming words.

You feel brain dead from the day. The family around you is bubbling away and chatting and wanting to share the day and you're sitting there brain dead. The thought of forming words or doing more than sitting on the couch and staring at the box seemed like scaling Mt Everest with a box of rocks on your back.

And then you got up and did it all again the next day.

I'm not complaining as the business was booming but you have to know when it's time for a holiday and stay fresh and keep your people happy.

After all, everyone on the other side of the bar is here for a holiday. They're out having a good time, you're the one working. So the less you make it seem like work, the more it seems like a holiday for your customers.

Cellar Door Visitors

There's an old Chinese saying that goes something like this:

He who cannot smile, should not keep shop

We found this very, very true.

The cellar door business started small and grew each passing week, month and year. You've seen the other sections about the bus tours, the festivals, weddings and other events.

For years and years we logged details about all our visitors. We kept a simple sheet of paper and wrote down all the details. How they found us, how they got here, how much they bought and what country they came from. It made fascinating reading and pretty soon you saw the patterns.

Any major event killed business during the event and then we'd be flooded afterwards. During the Olympic Games in Sydney we were dead quiet. But afterwards as people stayed in Oz and explored the country they came pouring in.

Australia is so far away from anywhere else in the world that people tend to stay longer and travel further while they're here. It's not like living in London and skipping over to France for the weekend. If you're living in Melbourne then France is at least a 24 hour flight away.

Another example was the Melbourne Cup week. During the week we were pretty quiet as people were busy doing Cup week stuff. And, since the room rates for major hotels shot up during Cup week we didn't get many other travellers. They all avoided Melbourne during peak price periods.

The same for the Grand Prix, Fashion Week, Super Bikes, the Garden Show, etc. You name it and we felt it. It probably sounds bizarre as you're reading this but we saw it every time. The events going on in Melbourne and even further away in Australia impacted our winery way out in the country. If you're out on holidays you probably don't really care what exact date you're going to be anywhere. By that I mean you don't really care if you see Melbourne on a Tuesday or a Thursday. If a week means the difference between $650 and $250 per night for the exact same room, I know which one I'm going to choose.

Straight after any major event we got the 'stay a while longer' travellers and the 'built up demand' other travellers, that is, the travellers who'd specifically not travelled due to this major event and the associated higher prices. You could set your watch by the traffic patterns.

After any major Aussie vs England sporting match we got the 'barmy army' stopping in and you'd be searching a long time to find nicer people. They were out here to enjoy themselves and they took that goal seriously. Some looked up long-lost relatives and dragged them out on the road to see some white lines. Others rented a campervan and set out to see Australia on their own. You could pick 'em walking in by the smile on their faces and lobster red suntans.

And every person stopping by had their own fascinating story. Who are they, what are they doing here, what do they want to see.

We got the backpackers and we got the NYC drug enforcement officer out on holidays. We got the professional tea taster from Sri Lanka and we got the trade union secretary from Shanghai (it was a she, not a he). You could write a book about the stories which I guess is part of what you're reading now.

For more cellar door business we put out a newsletter for many years and people loved it. I can't say we were snowed under by the sales coming from it but that was way before Facebook and Twitter and iPhones. It worked as a reminder for people to stop by and pick up their next dozen wines. Anyway, the key point is that it worked.

And you could have a fantastic time people watching at the cellar door. Some groups coming through were having a lousy day. They were disorganised, some of them were already trashed and they were simply having a miserable time. Other groups were having a ball and this was the best day they'd had in a while. We figured out what the 'good time' groups did and I wrote an article about it for the newsletter. I realise most of this sounds like basic common sense but you'd be amazed at the things we saw. Here's the article;

1 – Plan your trip and call ahead - You've got your winery map in front of you. So plan a route and be realistic about how long it'll take you to drive from winery to winery. Can you really cover 50km of twisty road in 30 minutes? Be honest about what you can do in 1 day and more importantly, what you can enjoy in 1 day. It's not a race to log the most tasting notes in 48 hours.

Stop...
Look...
Taste...
Listen...
Learn...

And most importantly enjoy the day.

Call each winery a few days before your weekend. Not all small wineries open every day and some close altogether over winter.

Plan your trip and leave time to enjoy your stay at each winery. About 1 hour should do.

2 – Line up a designated driver - You've probably already figured out where you want to stay the night. But you still need to get from winery to winery. Find someone who doesn't drink or is willing to not drink this one weekend. It's just plain easier and safer for you.

3 – Wear something comfortable and dark - For shoes, leave the stilettos and designer heels home this weekend. Wear something you're comfortable walking and standing in. Not every winery will have space for you to sit down so you may be standing most of the day.

And wear comfy dark clothes. Dark clothes hide whatever you or more likely someone else spills on you. And it's easier than having to change or walk around looking like Spot the dog for the day.

4 – Go easy on the after shave or perfume - A huge part of what you taste comes from the smell. That's why food always tastes flat when you've got a blocked nose. It's much easier to pick up the spice in the Merlot when you're not battling with the Old Spice from the person next to you.

5 – Have a decent breakfast and plan a good lunch - You'll stay sober longer and you'll get the best from your days away with a decent breakfast under your belt. It's no fun getting smashed by 11am on the first day when you've still got half a dozen wineries to visit.

Get a decent breakfast and leave time for a good lunch. Either bring your own picnic basket and eat out in the vines or eat in. If you've planned lunch at someplace small and far away then please book ahead. Often it'll be the only thing for miles and remember, plan ahead and you'll enjoy your weekend away much, much more.

6 – Get there early - We know, from experience that afternoons are busiest. So try and get out of home and be at the first winery bang on opening time. Whoever's behind the bar will have more time to spend with you, you'll have a better time and you'll learn more.

7 – Taste the wines in order of lightest and driest to strongest and sweetest - Tasting fine wines is just like enjoying a fine dinner. You start off with a light entrée and you finish with the sticky date pudding. Just imagine what your prawn cocktail tastes like after your ice cream? Start with the light whites and finish with the ports.

8 – Learn to spit - If you swallowed everything you tasted in one day on the road, you'd be hammered by lunchtime.
Learn to spit.
It's an accepted and expected thing to do in the wine world.
But please... practice at home first.

9 – Don't stress about taking tasting notes - Remember you're out to enjoy your weekend and your wines and not check the boxes on a score sheet. Grab the wines you like on the day (please keep them out of the boot on a 40C degree day). And get yourself on the winery mailing list. Most wineries will have a newsletter and tasting notes online so don't worry about scribbling notes that you'll probably lose on the way home. Once you're on the mailing list you can order your favourite wines anytime.

10 – Keep drinking water all day long - Sipping wines and travelling all day dries you out. Carry your water bottle with you, keep it topped up and keep sipping all day. It just means you keep tasting wines longer and don't flake out early on.

11 – What goes in, must come out - Use the toilets at each stop. I know it sounds obvious and we're not 3 years old anymore but we see all sorts of strange things. So stop at the loo whenever you get a chance.

12 – Enjoy they stay - Relax and go with the flow and just have a good time. Don't rush as it's not a race. If you don't get through your planned route, then so be it. There'll always be another weekend and hey, do you really need an excuse for another wine weekend away?

Remember... You'll be in a new area enjoying new things, new wines and meeting new people. Just kick back and enjoy the experience.

Loyalty Cards

At last count, I have loyalty or 'coffee' cards from my barber, grocery store, 3 coffee shops, bookshop, mechanic, catering supplier, salad bar, Thai restaurant and untold online sites.

So why couldn't I do one for my own customers?

We looked at a few different ways to do this. We thought about a software package where we'd scan our customers' card and the software kept track of purchases. We looked at RFID cards (like touch credit cards or door swipe cards) that you could brush past a reader to pick up the details. But in the end we settled for a normal business card, printed front and back and a $2 kid's stamp we had lying around.

And again it worked like a charm. We changed the design after a while but the basic, low-tech business card worked a treat.

For the drivers and guides who we saw every few weeks instead of every day, we kept their card behind the bar and stamped it for them. They'd often be rummaging in the coffee card basket finding their card while we were busy with their customers. They were grateful to pick up their bottles every few days and some of these guys built up pretty decent wine cellars. One poor guy didn't even drink but he was a great salesman so he ended up with a shelf full of wines and I'm sure his friends loved him.

Every card represents a dozen bottles at full retail price. And they were still pouring in (no pun intended) every day, all day.

Staff

If you've ever 'invested' in a racehorse you'll know the number 1 rule of horses: sooner or later they all go lame. And that was our experience with staff.

Don't get me wrong as we had the pleasure of working with a few world class people and some became lifelong friends. And at the other extreme there are people I really have to wonder about. How the hell do they survive in this world?

There's no shortage of management textbooks offering wonderful advice about employees and how to treat your staff and whatever…

The very real fact remains no matter how you dress it up: we owned the place, had bills to pay and a payroll to meet every week; everyone else worked there and didn't have any 'skin' in the game.

The people over 45 seemed to understand this and had the values and morals to turn up every day when they said they would and give their best. We had some fantastic 'over 45' people. They brought their experience, common sense, work ethic and sense of humour with them. They were a pleasure to be with and we laughed ourselves stupid more times than I can remember.

One guy came to us for a working 'holiday' after he'd spent many years running a high pressure hotel. He had more than enough qualifications and just wanted something a little slower and easier for a while. He was fantastic with people and had a wicked sense of humour and boy did he use it. I still smile every time I think of the times we had with this guy.

The people under 30 seemed to come from a different world. Nothing was ever their fault. When there were cows across the road and they got there 15 minutes late, guess what? It wasn't their fault. When the car wouldn't start and they turned up 2 hours late, guess what? It wasn't their fault.

The idea of leaving 10 minutes early just wasn't on their radar. The thought that they're working in a customer facing business and there might be a customer standing on the doorstep who doesn't care about your problems and just wants some wines seemed utterly incomprehensible to them. I know I'm sounding like the classic old fart carrying on how things were done in 'their' day, but the facts haven't changed. We were open to the public and you're only as good as your last interaction with your customer.

When I was having a bad day I still had to put on my Sunday best smile and front up. In your own winery when you're the face of it you can't have a bad day. It's you, the buck either starts or stops with you.

You can brush aside your bad day, hangover, whatever and get out there and make your payroll for the week. Or you can make excuses why you can't. Either way the payroll's still there at the end of the week.

It was our business and the only choice available was to take responsibility and make our business 'work'.

You can make excuses or you can make money.

When my twenty-something staff member called in sick at 9:50am (we opened at 10am) because they were out partying all night and couldn't be bothered coming in, it was me and my partner taking up the slack. Has anyone noticed the irony in this? I'm there to take the phone call for my staff calling in to say they can't make it?

Some of the excuses we got still make me laugh and feel sick at the same time. I guess the idea of being early for work so you can start on time died out a while ago but no one told the small business owners of the world.

We wrote a pretty extensive staff induction and training workbook. The aim was to give new starters a reference book on how the place ran and enough wine knowledge and history to get them started.

And it covered the really dog arse dumb sort of questions that could just chew up your time with no reward. One practical example of this was the message on the answering machine. We lost mains power regularly, the battery backups in the answering machines tended to last not very long at all and finally we fried more than a few answering machines due to lightning strikes. Being a tin shed on the top of a hill with power poles nearby attracted more than our fair share of lightning. So the really simple act of including a script for the answering machine saved me having to repeat this every second week. And it gave us a consistent message that answered most callers questions (the most asked was; what times are you open?) before we even got to call them back.

The real advantage to us was that no one could ever say we didn't tell them something. The manual laid out clearly what was acceptable, what was expected and what was not acceptable. It's 122 pages long and there are a lot of wine facts and local history in there so for some it was a lot of reading.

On the other hand were the real 'salt of the earth' people I had the absolute privilege of working with. Over the years we employed a fair few people doing the hard work out in the vineyard. They came, they went and I'll spare the details and offer the insight instead. I was utterly dumbfounded how many of these people were barely literate.

I read and write for a living and for me it's a little like breathing: we all do it. But when I asked some of my employees for a mobile number they'd take a scrap of paper from their wallets and I could see they were copying the characters and not remembering the numbers. These were wonderful, hardworking, honest as the day is long type folks, it's simply that for some reason the education system had failed them. Or they'd had to start work early in life and had missed the basic education we take so very much for granted. We were careful to never put them in a position to embarrass them but often you really had to stop and think through the consequences. If I've got someone spraying the vineyard for me and I leave a written spray chart, can they read enough to pick the mildew spray from the weed spray?

Am I getting fertiliser on my vines or herbicide?

And how would I know?

The answer was pretty simple: We left the right chemicals out with nothing else nearby. If there's only one thing in front of you, then it's the only thing you can use.

Clearly we took a different approach with our vineyard staff from our cellar door staff. Our vineyard staff didn't get the 122 page workbook for the obvious reason laid out above. It was pretty humbling to see this happening just 93km from the second largest city in Australia.

Amway Visit

Early 2004 saw global MLM Company Amway run their annual conference in Melbourne, Australia. Over 1,000 of Amway's high performers landed in Australia for the conference and then scattered to all the great tourist destinations around the country.

And since we were firmly entrenched in many inbound tourism operators schedules, Amway got a stop at the winery.

They had a full on camera crew recording the visit. I'm pretty certain the camera they used was worth more than my first house.

They all had a great time, Gippsland turned on a spectacular day for them and I'm sure they got some fantastic footage for their Aussie adventure feature film.

3 FUNCTIONS AT THE WINERY

Australia Day - Setup

The work to set up any festival was phenomenal. It's not something you throw together the night before and have 300 happy, entertained and well fed customers the next day.

We started planning 3 months out from the event and I'll give you an idea of what happened at what times.

About 2 months out we were ready with all our advertising and promotional materials. The main event running the 2 month period was Australia Post. We tested just about every promotional method you can think of and 3 items stood out - unaddressed mail delivery, banners on the roadside plus our email list worked best.

Australia Post required 6 weeks notification for a mail drop so that drove our timeframe.

We tested local newspaper adverts, local radio, Melbourne radio, flyers in the local area, posters in local businesses, signs on the roadside, etc. You name it, we tried it. And in the end the humble brochure going out to every mailbox in the area proved the best.

Big banners on the roadside lured in the daytrippers and the email list kept our wonderful faithful followers informed. But for repeatable, verifiable crowd pulling return per dollar, the local flyer worked best.

12 weeks out we knew the date, time, what we were doing on the day and started promoting it in the monthly email newsletter.

8 weeks out we knew what band we'd have on the day, what food we'd be preparing and our advertising plan (and content) was done.

6 weeks out we booked the mail delivery and started promoting it fulltime in the emails.

4 weeks out we had the printing done and we'd lined up our butcher and other catering folks. If we needed new banners for the roadside we'd be designing and making these now.

As a sad side note, the woman who made the best potato salad in the world died not long ago and took her recipe with her. We still have no idea what she did or how she did it or what she used but there was never ever any leftover potato salad.

3 weeks out we had the flyers lodged with the post office. We were counting down to the day with the gardens and lawns on track to look spectacular.

2 weeks out we were building up wine and soft drink supplies. All the staff, balloons, balloon gas and decorations were organised.

1 week out we stopped accepting bookings to finalise numbers on the day. We'd place final orders with our butchers and other caterers. The garden tents and chairs were coming out for a clean before the day. Any food we could prepare in advance we did. As the day got closer, every refrigerator in place was bulging out the sides.

If we knew we were finishing late and people would be leaving after sundown, we'd have the flood lights out and tested.

The days right before the event were busy. Any decorations we could put up, we did. Anything we could do early was done.

Australia Day - Our Guests

In all our years at the winery we've never had a single 'incident'. Some bars around town throw out drunks every night but we've never had so much as a heated argument with any customer, ever.

There's not much to talk about here other than to say that every person here supported us over the years. Some dropped in and became lifelong friends. Some we don't see anymore.

But that's life and that's how it goes.

Australia Day - The Food

This was another thing we tested over the years.

We tested BYO and we tested self serve and we tested paper plates vs real plates vs you name it, we tested it.

Our results show a fully catered meal with plenty to eat served on real plates with real cutlery worked best. By 'worked best' I mean raving 'so good they have to tell all their friends' customers giving us thumbs up feedback and buying lots of wines.

I'm not sure what the link is between paper plates and fewer wine sales but it's there. Whenever we've served meals on paper plates we've sold less wine. Go figure…

The BYO option was another interesting test. We tried putting on the band for free, selling the drinks and people bringing their own lunch. The reasoning was for people to save some dough and still have a great day out.

It was a dismal failure.

People didn't want to bring their own just to save a few dollars and what was worse, we sold less wine. They were coming along to be spoilt a little and enjoy a great day out with music, food, views and drink. The last thing they wanted was to wash up their own dishes.

People work hard and long in the country. Sitting in a comfy office thinking you're working hard is a long way from even a slow day out in the bush. A normal day on the farm would pretty much kill most people driving a desk for a living. I know it did me at first. So when country people party, they party good and cleaning your own dishes after a day out simply doesn't cut it.

We found it's the little things that make a huge difference in profitability. We set a cut-off date for bookings so we got accurate catering costs. The last thing you want is 25kg of cooked beef sitting in the fridge. The dog absolutely loved us when this happened but poochy's affection doesn't make the payroll.

We were nervous about numbers on the day for our first festivals and wondered if we'd get plenty of people. So we did anything possible to get the most number of people through the door and that meant we let people pay for the ticket on the day. But that left us either short or over with food. I realise any restaurant or takeaway joint faces this every day but we weren't doing this every day. For us it was a huge investment and the last thing we wanted was to lose money on the day rather than earning some.

Like most things we shouldn't have worried. No one batted an eyelid when we changed tack and asked for pre-paid bookings. Our customers did just that: they called, they emailed, they sent cheques in the mail, they dropped in at the cellar door and they bought their tickets. We knew our numbers for the day and everyone (except the dog) was happy.

And making it work in the day?

When people first arrived we had the 'book in' counter open. They came to the bar and we'd check them off the list. We'd hand them several chips, as in poker chips from a poker set which they'd present to collect their main meal, sweets, freebie drink or whatever. It worked well but we never, I repeat never, got back 100% of the chips we handed out on the day.

Australia Day - Raising the Flag

For the very first Australia Day festival many years ago we put in a brand spanking new flagpole and flew our first Australian flag. The wild winds and weather meant we got about six months from each flag. Then it was time for a new one.

We asked the Mayor of Bass Shire, Councillor John Hulley, to raise the first flag. He did and he's been a loyal supporter of the winery ever since.

When John Hulley's tenure ended we roped in the local member, Ken Smith MLA. Ken's raised the flag for us ever since and Ken comes with an added benefit. As the local member he has a yearly flag allowance which means he gets a number of flags to give away to his electorate. So Ken Smith not only raised the flag for us but he brought us a new flag every year.

And the lesson we learnt from this was to ask. Never, ever be afraid to ask anyone for anything. The worst that can happen is they say no.

We never imagined the local member would be a loyal guest and supporter year in, year out.

We never imagined the Mayor of the Shire would turn into a great friend who supported us then and in the years until the very end.

It was quite humbling to realise the respect and influence we had in the community.

It is very humbling.

Australia Day - The Band

You've probably figured out by now that we tested everything we could have tested and that included the music.

We tried no music, we tried a DJ, we tried folk singers and we tried bands.

Guess what?

They all worked really well.

We found our audience responded best to the mellow covers bands. People liked live music and would be up and dancing as soon as lunch was over. We found a DJ would get the youngies up and bopping but the oldies refused to play along. And since most of our audience had grey hair (us included) we did things to keep the most people happy.

The cost?

Yeah, it cost more to have live music, however our testing showed it was worth the additional spend. And we got lots more people turning up when we advertised a live band.

Australia Day - Behind the Bar

Life behind the bar went from quiet to frantic and back to quiet.

For our very first festivals we were nervous and edgy and going through all the emotions and questions. Have we got enough food, will plenty of people arrive, have we put away enough cold wines, will we, have we, did we…

We pretty quickly figured out what worked and what didn't. But, like most things, the first time's the worst.

Festival peak time was arrival time. That 45 minute stretch with folks streaming in for the 'well-advertised' start time was pure nuts. With all hands on deck, we still had people queued 5 deep.

And you know what? It was ok.

No-one ever stormed out in disgust over a 5 minute wait. No-one ever yelled and screamed. And no one ever lay on the ground kicking and screaming throwing a 2 year olds temper tantrum. I'm sure we were more worried and stressed than anyone else. But we still liked to get things 110% right for our people.

Check-in time meant we checked names off the booking list and gave everyone their bag of tokens for the meal and drinks. It sounds easy; however we were dealing with people who had supported us over many festivals, people we knew, friends from work, relatives, folks from the local area, new people coming from our adverts, you name it, people came and supported us. And everyone wanted a chat and some of our time which is so very important. Without talking to people and making the people connection, we'd still have been trading from a tiny tin shed. We would never have had the support if we hadn't.

It was just a shame we never had enough time to catch up with everyone on the day.

There's plenty of pictures with only a few people in front of the bar and very, very few when it was frantic. Probably for the very good reason that grabbing the camera when it was frantic was low on my list of things to do.

Australia Day - Afterwards

The time when everyone left and we were sitting in the quiet and dark was when the tired hit.

We'd spent weeks working towards this day and we were psyched and buzzing on the day and then the day came. And the day went and now it's the end of the day.

The mental and physical exhaustion kicked in at the end of the day and we were simply dog tired knackered. The downside was that you're absolutely stuffed but your mind's still going at 100 miles an hour. It's the stage of exhausted when you've got trouble forming words but you're still wide awake.

There's just no way you can sleep without a few glasses of red to slow the brain to match the body.

And that folks was a really good tired.

Bass Coast Christmas

The local Shire celebrated their Christmas party with us which was a great surprise.

Why was it a surprise?

Well, our shire includes the third most visited tourist attraction in Australia, the Penguin Parade. There's no shortage of top class, five star, four star, three star and no star places that'll host a function in a snap.

So why did they choose us?

Well, we supported the area a helluva lot. We spent local, we employed local and we supported local. We went out of our way to support local whatever we could. Supporting us was their way of saying thanks to us.

We catered the finger food and the Wonthaggi local brass band blew the afternoon away.

This support was great for us to get and it was a really, really nice feeling.

Car Clubs

The winery was on the main road running from Melbourne to Phillip Island. Phillip Island motor raceway hosts the Australian Moto GP, the World Superbikes and some other motor racing event pretty much every day of the year. So it's a popular destination for any car or bike club in Melbourne and we got our fair share: car clubs, rallies, outings, get togethers and even a car club AGM.

It was great to see these folks. And some of the cars they had were worth more than the first 3 houses I lived in.

But, they didn't drink or buy much wine, maybe because some of the cars were worth more than the first 3 houses I lived in…

Christmas Functions

Once the word got around we were a friendly, low cost (relatively in the area) venue, the function bookings started rolling in, especially around Christmas time.

And we saw everything. From the low cost, BYO BBQ picnic right up to the fully catered, entertainment for the kids and live band party.

A huge part of our success was our easygoing attitude with people. Folks come to a place to have a good time. Everyone has different expectations and different 'must haves' for their function. We fitted in with most of them.

If someone wanted to cater their own, that was fine with us.

If someone wanted us to cater everything for them, then that was fine as well.

We put together a functions 'check list' on the website listing things for people to think about before they book a venue.

It worked super well and here's what it said:

Functions

If you're after a great value no stress function in a stunning location looking out over the water while staying on budget and having everyone rave about it for a long time, then read on...

We've hosted a lot of weddings, birthday parties, engagements, hen's nights, Christmas parties and festivals at the winery. And you can split these into 2 types of functions.

Type 1 is where everyone has a good time. The function runs smoothly, on time, on budget and the organiser has a fantastic night with everyone telling her what a great time they've had.

And then there's the type 2 functions. Things are missing, people are late, it costs more than expected, the guests have a lousy time and the organiser is off in the corner crying.

Thankfully we have very few type 2 functions.

To help you have the most stress free, best organised, most talked about function ever, here's the top ten rules to follow. They may seem like a lot of work but... There is a reason for all this planning.

The more you do before the day, the better time you'll have on the day because the old saying still holds true:

'Failing to plan is planning to fail...'

1. Is this the right venue for you?

If you've got 50 people coming for a casual birthday party, they'd be very uncomfortable and feel out of place in a grand ballroom designed to hold 200. Likewise, trying to squeeze 120 people into a function room built for 50 won't make you any friends.

Match the venue to your function and your guests. If you're planning a casual day, go for a casual venue with finger food or a buffet meal. Silver service will just make everyone nervous and feel lousy.

Get your invitations out early and give your RSVPs time to respond so you'll have accurate guest numbers. This will greatly help you with catering and drinks costs. The best organised functions tell us 2 weeks in advance exactly how many people they'll have on the day.

Remember the band or DJ. Is there room for them? When the venue says it seats 120, does this mean you have to move tables to get to your dance floor. If you have to turn down the music since you're blasting the table of honour, it'll kill the mood and you won't have many people up and rocking away. Decide on what you want and check the details.

The Gurdies Winery holds up to 100 people for sit down or stand-up finger-food functions. There is plenty of space out in the gardens and on the deck overlooking the bay. And there's plenty of space for the band…

2. Location, location, location…

Can everyone find and get to your function? The Surprise goes out of the Surprise Party when your guests walk in at the same time as the guest of honour because they couldn't find the place. And we've seen functions where key guests or family members arrive an hour late due to poor directions.

The best run functions we've seen send all their guests a map and clear written directions on how to get here.

You'll also find that any guests driving for 2 or more hours will want to stay nearby so look for a local accommodation directory.

The Gurdies Winery is 70 minutes from Melbourne CBD, 30 minutes from Phillip Island, 40 minutes from Cranbourne, 30 minutes from Pakenham, 15 minutes from Kooweerup and just 10 minutes from Lang Lang, Pioneer Bay, Corinella, Coronet Bay, Loch, Kernot and Grantville. There is plenty of parking onsite and click here to see accommodation in the area.

We have a hi-res map and clear instructions for you to download and use. Email me and we'll get these to you.

3. Working with the people and looking over the venue

You need to be comfortable when dealing with the people at the venue. Do you 'click' with them or do they make the hairs on the back of your neck stand up? It's your day and you want a great day so the last thing you need are hassles with the venue. Here's just a few of the basic questions to ask:

- Visit the venue, walk around, talk to the functions director and inspect the room you'll be using on the day. If you don't like it or them, move on... There are plenty of other places out there that'll be more than happy to talk to you.
- Ask about the catering. Can you bring in your own caterers or do you have to use the catering offered by the venue?
- Ask about dropping off the cake or your special dish early. Is there fridge space or a cool room to store your foods?
- Ask about the drinks. Do you get discount rate drinks or are you paying full retail? Can you set a limit on the bar tab?
- And if the party's rocking and everyone's having a great time, can you extend the bar limit or are you locked in?
- Are the setup and pull down times flexible? Can you get in the day before to put up your decorations or do you have to rush in 30 minutes before the guests arrive?
- Are you expected to clean up the venue or do you just walk away at the end of the night?

Ask all these basic questions while you're looking around and it'll save you time and pain.

The Gurdies Winery gives you the choice; your caterers are free to use our kitchen or we can recommend some outstanding caterers we regularly work with.

You can drop off your cake or distinctive dish or even special drinks a few days early. They'll be safe and icy cold when you're ready to go.

We have our wines and other drinks at function prices and you can set a bar tab for whatever limit you wish. We'll let you know when the limit's getting close so you can decide to stick with your budget or keep going.

You're free to come and go and setup for your function before hand. Depending on where you setup in the winery, there are people coming to the cellar door during the day so keep that in mind.

Now that you've decided on the function venue and where, check out these details that'll make all the difference for your big day.

4. The type of Function or Event

Decide on the 'theme' and time of your function. This one decision will have the greatest impact on your catering and function costs. Is it informal nibbles, cocktail food, buffet 'sit anywhere' or sit down silver service?

Is the venue supplying the catering or do you want your own caterers?

The time of day will impact how hungry your guests are. A 10am or 3pm function will need less food than a 1pm or 6pm function. A 60th surprise party at 10 am or 3pm will eat and drink a whole lot less than an engagement party at 12 noon or 7pm.

Have you catered for the vegetarians, the diabetics, the allergy sufferers? The easiest way to find this information is to ask for it on the RSVP. Ask people if they have any special dietary requirements, it really is that easy.

The Gurdies Winery works with you to make sure you have a great function. We're flexible and we work with you before, during and after the event to make sure you have a great function. And we're happy to give you feedback on your ideas. We've seen a lot of things that work well and more importantly, we've seen the things that don't work well.

5. Decide on your budget and priorities and stick to them

Have some idea of your budget before you speak to your venue. This includes the menu selection, the wines, the beers, what you leave 'on the counter' as your drinks tab, the decorations and the band or DJ.

If you ask anyone about the last great function they went to they'll probably say it had 'heaps of top food, great music and a good atmosphere'. A year or two later no one's going to remember the sterling silver candle holders or the matching custom printed napkins and balloons. Put your money where it matters and keep your guests happy. They'll love you for it.

The Gurdies Winery has options for all budgets, including yours.

6. Entertainment

Check out your entertainment. If you can't see them perform somewhere else, get a demo CD or DVD. Some people look great on the website and that's where they should stay as they're pretty ordinary in real life. Make sure they can play the sort of music you want and what your guests will want to dance to.

And, ask them if they're happy for you to use their microphone for your speeches. It will save you a lot of hassle having to arrange your own PA.

The Gurdies Winery can recommend bands, DJs or even juke boxes for hire. Let us know what you're after and we can help.

7. Wet Weather Options

The best run and best fun functions we've seen have a wet weather plan. The catering and entertainment are the easy things. Think about your photo sessions. If you have older guests then think about how quickly they can get from the car park to the venue. Do you have some big umbrellas to help them? Do you have to carry gifts or cakes from the car? If you've got your heart set on an outside function, can the band setup inside somewhere?

Just stop and think about what happens when it's raining.

The Gurdies Winery has plenty of space under cover. Even if you've planned to have 100 people sitting outside next to the vines, there's plenty of room under cover.

8. Planning and scheduling

Have a plan for the event and a schedule of when things happen.

The best example of this is a surprise party. You want all your guests there to sing and clap when the guest of honour arrives. Generally older guests will arrive way early and younger guests will arrive late. Telling your 70th surprise party guests to arrive a half hour early will see most of them there an hour before. Telling your 25th birthday surprise party guests to arrive an hour before will see most of them there 15 minutes after the event. That's just how it works.

Start your music at the time listed on the invitation and make sure the band or DJ knows the schedule of events. They will work their 'sets' around your photos, speeches, videos, presentations, raffles, dinner etc.

The last thing you want with people rocking on the dance floor is to stop everything, turn up the lights and draw a raffle.

Likewise, when the bride and groom disappear for the photos, think about the music, drinks and nibbles for your guests. Because you're busy doesn't mean they are and a half hour is a very long time staring at your feet.

The Gurdies Winery works with you to make sure you have a great function. We're flexible and we work with you before, during and after the event to make sure you have a great function. And we're happy to give you feedback on your ideas. We've seen a lot of things and that work well and more importantly, we've seen the things that don't work well.

9. Seating plan

Think about your guests when you're doing the seating plan. You'll know who you can sit where without family feuds. But there are other things to think about.

Don't put your older guests right next to the speakers as they'll get blasted by the music. Put the people you know will be up and rockin' at the loudest table. If you're doing the seating plan and you don't know who these people are, then make some calls and find out.

Have a kids table and put someone in charge. Provide some entertainment for the kids such as colouring books, entertainment or games. This'll keep the kids happy and quiet, it'll let mum and dad have a great time and it'll let everyone on the dance floor have a top time without fretting about knocking over a stray little person.

The Gurdies Winery provides a venue map so you can plan you seating, your gift table and your band. Email me and we'll get this to you.

10. A Happy Ending

Most bands and DJs book for a 4 hour minimum. Check the band's policy and more importantly the venue's policy on going overtime. If everyone's rocking along and the mood is great and the band starts to play Auld Lang Syne…. Well then a nod and a wink to the band might get you another hour of music but only if you've arranged it before hand. Most bands or DJs plan their song list and like to finish 'big'. So the best time to let the band know is about 30 minutes before the scheduled finish time. This gives them time to shuffle their song list so they can keep everyone up and dancing and still finish on a high note.

And if the band says yes and the venue says no, well then you've got a new problem. Ask about the liquor license and partying on later. Is the venue licensed past this time? What will it cost you for the venue to go overtime? And what does it do to your carefully planned budget?

Do your homework about going overtime and it'll make it easy to decide 'on the spot'.

The Gurdies Winery is licensed till late and the bands and DJs we recommend are happy to keep playing while people are dancing.

I had to go to the original winery website to get the 10 point list above. I've sent this out to hundreds if not thousands of people. The site has had tens of thousands of hits on this page alone.

And know what?

I still found some typos.

How embarrassing is that?

But it still worked, typos and all.

I took out the typos I could find before using it here.

Local Meetings

For some of the early meetings we still had the old winemaking stuff scattered around the place and the pallets of bottles stacked next to the speaker's table.

Not ideal, but people loved the atmosphere.

We had a very basic kitchen and I have to give credit where it's due: the local health inspector was not only realistic, but had some great practical ideas on how to do things cheaply and efficiently.

Easter Harvest Festival - Setup

We started the Easter Harvest festival and in later years invited the other wineries in our road to join in.

The format of the harvest festival was different to our other festivals. Rather than a catered event running from lunchtime until evening, we encouraged a 'drop in and have a look around' atmosphere. There were plenty of other things happening in the area over the Easter break so we aimed to get the people already in the area or driving past to stop, come in and have a look around. They would (hopefully) stop a while, have something to eat, listen to the music and buy some wines.

There's a famous line from the movie "Field of Dreams", it was something like 'build it and they will come'.

What a load of crap.

You build it and then the real work starts and you promote it and you advertise it and you spend every waking minute pushing your own venue and then you'll get the people.

Sure, you build the relationships and you build the reputation and you'll get the repeat business. But that all takes time and effort and resources and passion and persistence.

What looks like an overnight success really is 15 years of hard work making it happen, not hoping it'll happen by magic.

A small winery sells its wines 1 bottle at a time. I'm sure there's ways to sell 10,000 bottles at a time, but we could never crack a large local order or export market, no matter how hard we tried.

But what we could do was get 1,000 ways to sell 1 bottle. You're reading about some of them here and now.

The statistics for small wineries are pretty damning. In fact if you look past the small winery statistics and look at small business statistics they overlap pretty well. The world just doesn't care about you even if do have the best winery, bakery, motel or mousetrap in the universe.

You, and only you, the owner and soul and life of your business have to get out there and hound people until they come and love your mousetrap or pinot or cabernet or whatever as much as you do. No one can replace the passion you have for your business.

It's up to you to make it happen.

No one else.

Easter Harvest Festival - Our Guests

With the harvest festival you never knew who'd be walking in the door next. We had our list of faithful supporters who turned up for each and every event. This included a lot of locals who were proud to claim us as their 'local' winery and showed us off to their city-folk relatives and friends.

But the harvest festival pulled in a wider crowd. We had events like the grape stomping and other attractions so it brought in different people.

Some people saw the banners on the roadside and stopped by for a few minutes.

Some others came and settled in for the day.

Easter Harvest Festival - Grape Stomping

We started this as a novelty event and created a monster.

We made a competition from this.

3 grape bins on the ground with 50kg of grapes in each and 3 teams of 4 people. Each team had to jump in, crush the grapes and the first to have a wine bottle full of juice won the game.

With an alcohol prize involved we had to have at least one adult involved. What we should have specified is that we needed to have at least one kid involved as the adults were muscling the kids out to get in the action.

We built the contest up, we had the commentary happening over the sound system and we had 3 sticky happy teams. You've never seen 12 people jumping up and down, slipping and sliding like their life depended on it to win a wine bottle. And people took this so very seriously. They were perched on the sides, muscles tensed, bare feet ready to go. We thought the big kids might crush the little kids but the little kids were just a keen to go as the big kids. Once the competitive factor kicked in it was free-for-all and less than a minute later we had our winner.

What we didn't figure on was the attractor factor of this. The kids (big and little) were in and out of the grape bins all afternoon. Some kids were coated head to toe in sticky, sweet grape juice. I'm not sure how the parents got them home or what state the car was in, but they loved it.

And people kept coming back to the bins all afternoon. They'd jump back in, they'd poke and prod and take photos and taste and ….

Clean up was pretty easy. Tip the bin out, then run the mower over it the next day as there wasn't that much left by the end of the day.

And every year afterwards we had people calling the winery asking if we were doing the grape stomping. I'm sure people came along for that one event.

Easter Harvest Festival - Easter Egg Hunt

We always added something new to each festival.

For the Cup day and Australia Day festivals we had trophies for things like: who brought the most people with them (45 was the record), the furthest travelled to get here (Sweden was the furthest we ever got) or even the best hard luck story for the day (a young couple were renovating their home and had a sewer pipe burst above their freshly renovated bedroom, they closed the door, called the builder and went away for the weekend).

It was something else to add value and get some laughs and make the day more memorable for our visitors.

Part of the harvest festival was the Easter egg hunt for the kids. Simple, easy and the kids loved it.

The ground was so dry for so many years. Australia had 6 years of continual drought from 2003 through until 2009 and we lived through all of them.

We had to hide the chocolate eggs in the vines and then quickly round up the kids for the hunt. Otherwise they started melting and that's no fun. And, if you left the eggs out long enough the magpies started carrying them off as they loved the bright shiny foil.

Such are the hazards of life in the country…

Easter Harvest Festival - The Band

We tried all sorts of bands and DJs and music. We never got great feedback from our customers about jazz bands, but when we had the harvest festival at the winery down the road, people raved about the jazz band. Go figure.

We found live music got people to take notice and it got them to come and see our place and get out of the house for the day.

Live music simply works.

We were paying out some serious dollars for a band and unless we sold a lot of wine on the day, we were going to be out of pocket. If we had a rainy or cold day, we would have lost money and been eating sausages for weeks.

Thankfully in all the years we ran festivals we never, not once, got rained out. I'm sure the gods were smiling on us while we were there.

Even for our catered festivals with pre-sold tickets where we knew we had our costs covered, the margins were still pretty slim. I'm not saying this in any way to discourage you if your dream is to own and run your own winery. I'm reporting to you on how we went, what we did and how it worked for us over the 18 years we owned the winery. For some people a few thousand dollars is worth the work, for others it's a complete and utter waste of time. Some wineries we compared notes with concentrated on wholesale markets, others aimed at the restaurants, some went the super-premium route, while still others exported their wines. And they all succeeded as did we.

But that knot in the stomach was still there before every festival. It was still there when we were scanning the weather report every day before the event. It was there each time a deadline came up on ticket sales and it was there right up until the very last person drove off the property.

Was it a stressful time? Yeah.

Was it a life changing experience? Most definitely.

Have I got the scars to prove it? Plenty of 'em: some emotional, some financial and some physical.

Have I met some of the finest people on this planet? Absolutely yes.

Was it worth it?

Oh yeah, I've got memories for a lifetime.

Greg Hunt Walk

Greg Hunt is our local MP, that's our Member of Parliament. Greg was a great supporter of ours and he was also a great publicist. He knew the value of having his photo in the paper every week and keeping in front of people. He never missed a chance to drum up some publicity.

One of his works was a fundraiser walk through his electorate where he did just that, he walked right through his electorate. Down every major road and up and down some pretty minor roads as well. And conveniently, right past the winery as well.

The local party faithful arranged a fundraiser at the winery while he was around. It had all the usual local character where everyone brings a 'plate'. That could be a warm meal, soup, desserts or whatever. All the local folks chip in to make it a great night out as the country can be a lonely place at times. The drive to your local bar can be a long one and events like this get people out and mixing in their area on a weeknight.

The thing that I want to highlight to you here is a really great and simple idea that I've used many times since.

We had a laundry basket full of raffle tickets and a table full of dozens and dozens of prizes.

Sure, some of the prizes are pretty simple, such as a little pot plant, but they're still prizes. The beauty of this super simple model, that is lots of little prizes, is that everyone with a raffle ticket in their hand walks out the door with a prize.

No one feels left out on the night.

No one goes home empty handed.

Think about the usual raffle at a fundraiser. There's one major prize and maybe two or three other prizes. Everyone buys a handful of tickets at the door when they walk in, but only two or three people walk out with a prize. And that's fine if you're in town and the major prize is a new car. But we're talking about a small community in the country with not a lot of social life.

Stop and take note and think about this the next time you're involved with a raffle.

Lots and lots of little prizes makes for lots and lots of happy people.

Party Fundraiser

We hosted many local fundraisers especially local political ones Plus a local guy brought his vintage car up. And for a fee, you could have your photo taken sitting in the car with your local politician of choice. Yeah, I'm sure some of you are laughing right now but, it worked. Everyone knows they're here for a few hours and they know they're going to leave with their wallet a little lighter. If we can put a smile on their face in some way, no matter how corny, then we've succeeded for the day.

The food was pretty simple, just snags on the BBQ and basic salads, but no one was there for a gourmet meal. They were there to support their cause.

The fundraiser folks were happy as they made several hundred dollars from their day out. And for them, they were happy with that. There's only so much spare money going around in a small community and every cent counts.

But for the winery, if we look at events like this purely on the costs vs returns for the day, it's a dead loss.

We had setup times, we had catering costs, we had clean up times and we needed additional staff as, while the fundraiser's happening, the usual business still goes on. Plus I couldn't really wander off and do something else that's been nagging me for weeks. We had to be there and we had to play host. Otherwise why would people come back to you?

But if you look at this as a long term investment in your business, then days like this are worth every single second. And they're valuable in a subtle way that wasn't really obvious when we started at the winery. It's the repeat business we got and it's the word of mouth business that we got that made it a fantastic day all round.

If everyone had a great day, they went out and told everyone they spoke to.

I lost count of the function bookings we got where the conversation started with:

Such and such was up there last week/month/year and they said they had a great time, do you take bookings for....?

Our repeat and word of mouth business was worth its' weight in 98 pinot noir.

And the other intangible for the day was the stories. I met and now know people living in the area way longer than I've been alive.

You can still see the indents in the neighbours paddock where the bullock teams trudged in supplies many years ago. There's a lot of history that's written only in people's minds. It's a shame so much of it will be lost, but that's how it is. There's a living history book out there and we're losing more and more pages every year.

Melbourne Cup Day Festival - Our Guests

Melbourne Cup Day in Melbourne fall around the start of November. For us that's still early in the growing season as you can see. The vines have some leaf on them but not a whole lot.

Cup Day was a strange festival for us. In Australia it's the horse race that stops a nation. In Melbourne it's a public holiday. In the rest of the country most workplaces stop to watch the race on the nearest television set.

The race itself is amazing. The prestige, the celebrations and the partying start weeks before and the hangover lasts for weeks afterwards. You see people wandering through the centre of Melbourne in their finest along with the usual business crowd. People go wild during Cup week and dress to the nines. Sure, there's the yobbos in the Flemington Course car park but there's also the A list in the members' stands.

We had our own A list crowd and they were all our customers. Some were more A list than others and they were the people who supported us at all our festivals.

I just want to stress again how important these people were and how glad we were for their support.

Melbourne Cup Day Festival - The Band

I've written about the bands in the Australia Day and Harvest Festival sections so I won't repeat the details.

One band, however, really sticks in my mind.

It was a band called "The Lovebugs" and they were terrific. They put on an awesome show, they rocked through a fair few brackets and their costume changes blew our people away. They got everyone up and bopping and had an unbelievable range of songs. And they sounded great too.

I guess they're the 2 main criteria we had for a successful band: our customers loved them and they were easy to deal with.

They weren't cheap but it's like anything in life where you get what you pay for.

We never got to use them again. Whenever we wanted them they were already booked with another gig.

Melbourne Cup Day Festival - Clean Up

Clean up's the time we were on autopilot putting away the things we could and trying to relax after the build up and hard work. Sure we left some clean up for morning but it was nice to get it mostly done the night before.

Some functions finished after midnight while some were done by 7pm. By midnight we were buggered. It had been an incredibly long day as we were usually out and about by 7am on festival days. There was so much to do each time and we couldn't afford to delay.

So the facial expression at the end of the day is a cross between exhaustion and elation.

Corporate Functions

Here's another example of an afternoon function. A section from one of the big banks wanted a relaxing afternoon fundraiser.

They supplied their own food, the band, the transport and the audience.

We put up the marquees and provided the venue. And, we gave them a cheque at the end of the day as part of the price of every bottle sold we donated back to the fundraiser.

So for us it was some new customers who remembered the spectacular views and beautiful sunny day.

For the people it was a chance to relax and enjoy time out with folks they usually see only in a work environment.

For the corporate customer?

Well, they got a great venue and no fuss.

Remember the usual business goes on in the background; this is another event happening at the same time. So we called in 1 of our regular people to stay for an afternoon shift to help with the other people coming in.

Convicts over the Wall

Every month or so a new tour operator stopped in as they were out scouting the countryside for new tour routes. Most new operators, and I really do mean 98% plus, we never saw again. We knew most of the drivers heading towards the penguin parade so we knew they weren't merely avoiding us. Their business plans simply didn't stack up. Margins in the tour business were tight and if you didn't have consistent bums on seats bookings year round then finances looked sick pretty quickly.

One ambitious fellow arrived with a TV show pilot and tour company proposal. His idea was to have 'convicts over the wall'. The story followed two 18th century escaped convicts and their escapades around the country. It was your standard lifestyle travel show with a slightly different twist.

They liked our place and we agreed to a 'convicts over the wall' festival day at the winery. We organised the other wineries in St Helier Road to come along and promoted the festival to draw in the crowds. The 'convicts over the wall' people brought along their camera crew who then ran riot through the vines and festival. They interviewed and filmed anything that talked and looked good.

Eventually we saw the first pilot and it was pretty good. But that unfortunately was the last we saw of the TV series, the tour company and the people involved.

By this stage we were pretty good at putting together a festival and pulling 300 people out of the woodwork.

We saw many small tour companies come and go. And only a tiny percentage lasted more than a few months. Those who did last supported us for many years.

4 GETTING MARRIED IN THE VINES

Setup

Wedding setup time was a little different from the festival setup. After the first few festivals, and the initial panic, we figured out what worked and what didn't. From there it was a case of 'rinse and repeat' and we were right to go. Sure we changed things around like catering and music and so on, but the basic structure was in place.

But the weddings were different because each one was utterly different from the next.

Some folks were fine with us catering finger food. We made the food then we donned our cleanest winery polo shirt and the black slacks with the least wine stains on them and we were the waiters for the evening. Other wedding parties wanted us there to keep an eye on the bar and that was it. No other involvement.

The variety of requests was stunning. The range of the requests was stunning. Every other wedding venue owner/manager I've spoken with had their set wedding 'pack'. This is what they offered and this is what they charged and this is what the customer got. We had the flexibility to work with the customer and offer something that was NOT a package deal. And that's how we attracted a big chunk of our business.

The upside was the customer got what they wanted and we got a lot more word of mouth referrals from happy customers. The downside was that each one was different. Completely and utterly and totally different in every way possible that you could ever imagine.

The first few weddings had us biting our nails waiting for the guests to arrive. We had no hospitality industry experience before we started the winery. My wedding experience was limited to being drunk at most of them.

And you know what?

We survived the first one and we got better and better, and we learnt from each one we hosted. I can't say it ever got to be routine but we got pretty bloody good at it. Every couple married at the winery thanked us and thanked us over and over again. Many have come back again and again and it is so very nice to see happy people together.

A key point I've grown to realise is how to avoid the 'conceit of outside knowledge'.

Just because you love eating out a lot doesn't mean you can run a restaurant.

Just because you love coffee doesn't mean you can run a coffee shop.

Just because you love wines doesn't mean you can run a winery.

As you've read here we struggled a lot during the early years and at times during our final years. We made a lot of mistakes but we survived and we thrived. But it took a lot of hard work to get there. We had a dream and we followed it and we followed it at a time when the barrier to entry in the wine industry was a lot lower than it is today. We loved our wines so in our naivety we thought we could do better. Sure, in some things we ended up doing better but it took close to 20 years and several million dollars. Offering opinion on something when you're an outsider is the easiest thing in the world and one of the worlds most popular pastimes. How many armchair sports coaches do you know? And how many successful real life coaches making a living from coaching do you know? Now let's say you've just been appointed manager of your favourite team. Who are you going to listen to for coaching advice? Someone who's watched 10,000 games and has an opinion on every move, play, ball and position ever played or someone who's successfully done the job? Someone sitting on the side lines or someone with skin in the game?

Would you take marriage counselling advice from someone who's been married and divorced 4 times or from someone happily married for 30 years?

Would you take financial management advice from someone up to the eyeballs in debt and desperate to make a sale or from someone who's retired early and is happily living off their investments?

After my experiences I'm much more careful who I listen to. Opinions are like arseholes - everybody's got one. But are they worth listening to? Well, now I'm pretty careful to suss out what success my opinion givers have had before listening to a word they say.

And if you're ever hosting a dinner party and have the need for 120 oyster forks, just call at your local winery. They've probably got at least that many laying around waiting for the next function…

Weddings were a great income for us. Sure it was a lot of work to setup and sure we were there till the wee hours and the clean up the next day was a drag, but it was regular income and we always got the flow-on business.

I've said this before and I'll keep repeating it because it happened all the time. People saw what we were doing and said we were lucky and we were an 'overnight success'. But what they didn't see was 18 years of consistent applied effort to be an 'overnight success'. I'm sure there was some luck in all of this; however the more work we did to be in a position to take advantage of an opportunity when it came along, the 'luckier' we got.

Are you lucky that you can say yes to host and charge for weddings when people ask. Or are you just prepared and working on your plan to have the buildings and gardens in shape so people want to have their wedding at your winery?

There's a lot to be said for consistency and having a plan and working towards that plan so you can be 'lucky' when the opportunity knocks.

One of the more unusual wedding requests was for fireworks. The customer said they'd supply their own, they wanted to know if we had any problems with them setting them off on the property.

At this stage we had the mental image of a few sparklers or roman candles on the lawns. What we didn't know was that some close family friend owned the largest fireworks distribution business in the southern hemisphere. The winery was in the middle of working farmland so we rang the immediate neighbours to warn them in case they had stock they we worried about.

The first time we were worried was when the fireworks guy arrived with a truck. When he casually told us he'd need a few hours to setup we really started to worry. The display lasted around 20 minutes and it was spectacular. These people had a beautiful clear night, the air was still, all the guests lined the railings watching the fireworks with the water shimmering in the background.

It was an unforgettable night.

The downside was one farmer a long way away ringing frantically to abuse us about scaring their alpacas. And, people from 5km away later told us they'd loved the show.

So was it a win or a loss? I don't know. The customer was happy, we had an awesome evening, we kept a lot of the locals happy with a free firework show and annoyed 1 person.

One thing I will concede blind luck to is the weather. We were outstandingly lucky with the weather. In all the years of hosting weddings we had one, I repeat one single one, wet weather day wedding. And even then the ceremony was sunny but straight after the clouds came over and the rain started up again. Yes, I'll concede that happy record to the weather gods.

Many, many people passed through our doors and we made a lot of friends and we sold of lot of wines and we saw many happy weddings.

And yes, it was a lot of long hard work to make it happen.

Silver Service

Amongst all the wedding requests we got to host only one full silver service wedding. We had formal, we had informal, we had a lot of combinations but we only ever got one silver service meal.

I'll digress for a moment.

Every caterer we've ever dealt with, except one, has been fantastic to deal with. They've always fed the band, they've fed us behind the bar, they've been organised, no fuss and easy to deal with. Just solid and good and professional and friendly people to deal with.

Except for one.

The exception was one 'silver service' wedding. The food was great, the place settings were spectacular and the guests had a wonderful time. From the customer perspective it was all they'd hoped for when they'd engaged this company.

But the ignorant 'individual' running the catering company was a nightmare to work with.

Everything was difficult and I won't go into the detail, but some things stood out. It was a hot summer afternoon and while my people didn't get a stale crust of bread from them, we were expected to provide unlimited drinks… And the list goes on.

It was a shame to see this.

The main thing was the customer had a top night.

For us, it was simply a shame to see this behaviour from supposed professional people when there is no excuse or need for it.

One dud experience in 18 years is not a bad record.

5 WINERY DOG

Jade, our yellow Labrador, grew up at the winery and now she's retired from the public eye. Her days are a little more relaxed now that she has time to enjoy her retirement at her city home.

If there was a way to track how many tourist photos Jade appears in, I'm sure it'd make the most popular YouTube video pale into insignificance. She was a star with the visitors and she never failed to play up to it. Labradors are people loving creatures and this one had the charm factor turned up to max. She also had the Labrador food scavenging factor running on overdrive.

Whenever there was a BBQ or picnic happening Jade would position herself next to her new found friends and play the big brown eyes and soft floppy ears for all they were worth. During the festivals we'd see her waddling back to the house after stuffing down who knows how many sausages and other leftovers.

For many years some tour companies used us as their lunchtime stopover. They brought along all their own sandwiches and used our kitchen for their tea and coffee.

The dog knew the sound their buses made.

She would be sound asleep in the house, sit bolt upright and then sprint out the door. She had heard one of the lunchtime buses chugging up the hill and wanted to be at the cellar door to greet them.

The road was about 1km from the house but, when it comes to Labradors and food, 1km doesn't present much of a difficulty.

She knew the routines of the winery and she knew the seasons. She knew which drivers and guides were good for a pat and which ones didn't much care for her. She had the whole thing figured out a lot sooner than we did.

Now she spends her days semi-retired reliving her younger hunting and running days in her dreams.

Unusual and Random

The winery lay east of Westernport Bay. Most nights were pretty good sunsets but some nights were simply jaw dropping. Different seasons saw the sun set over different parts of the bay and we had front row seats for it every single day. The bushfire season threw up plenty of dust and smoke into the air and this made the sunsets even more storybook.

Speaking of dust. We lived through one of Australia's longest droughts from 2003 until about 2009 (give or take a bit) so we got more than our fair share of dust storms. One day saw the dust so thick the sun looked like the moon at night trying to get through the dust.

One side effect of the dust storms was the water filters clogging. The winery was on tank water. We got irrigation water from the dams, the drinking water came from water tanks off all the buildings. A pump and filter provided water pressure into each building. A few days after the next rain following a dust storm the pumps would slow to a trickle and I'd be scratching my head: why all at once? The dust settled on the roofs, the rain washed the dust into the tanks where it settled to the bottom and got sucked into the pumps. The process took a few days so at first the cause and effect wasn't obvious and it was no big deal, we simply changed filters. But it was another one of those things to keep your eye on and another task to take care of to keep the place humming along.

Then there was the complete opposite. When it finally rained we thought about building another ark. The tanks were full, the dams filled and outdoor works stubbornly stayed undone.

And the smell. The smell of Mother Earth taking a drink from the first rain after a long dry is unforgettable. The earthy heady mix slams your senses to the point where you simply stand and stare at the rain pelting down. The temperature plummets, the dust disappears and rivulets run down the dirt that was lawn at some time in the past. The next day the green starts to sprout from every place. Mother Nature is geared to survive the booms and the busts. As soon as that precious water hits any seed lying in the ground, the seed knows what to do. The first flecks of green start popping up almost in front of your eyes. It's something that you never really see in the city. I count myself amongst the luckiest people on this earth that I've had the chance to see Mother Nature at her finest and close up for all these years.

The kangaroos? They were everywhere. When you were out at dawn or dusk you'd see them grazing on the fresh cut grass. We mowed acres and acres of lawns and as the fresh shoots came back, the roos thought it was heaven on a stick. And wouldn't you? If you got fresh new food delivered to your door every day, you'd be happy…

As it got drier and drier the roos came closer and closer to the buildings. I'd wander out in the morning and there'd be fresh roo poo at the kitchen door. I'd wake in the middle of the night to hear them munching and grunting by the bedroom window. It drove the dog nuts and she'd start barking at 2:32am, but that's what dogs do.

The roos had their own social structure as well. You could see who was the king roo and who were the pups. King roo was always a little away from the mob and besides being the boss, he was chief watchdog. At the first noise or movement he'd stand bolt upright and survey the scene. If danger (me or the dog) was still around, then he'd grunt at his mob, they'd hop off and last of all king roo would slowly hop after them. They're beauti. animals perfectly adapted to the Australian environment and seeing them was a real bonus.

6 THE WINES

We inherited shiraz, cabernet sauvignon, riesling, chardonnay and pinot noir vines and wines. We paid for the wines and we inherited the vines is a more correct summary.

We then planted merlot, more chardonnay, more riesling and verdelho which are covered in the planting new vines section.

The philosophy behind the wines was simple: we made clean, low-preservative wines that we liked to drink.

It was that simple.

Our passion, attention to detail and consistency resulted in a loyal following. People loved the low-preservative approach. The 'one-off' overseas tourists who liked the wines and bought a bottle or two to take home couldn't quite pin down what they liked about the wines. But like them they did.

Now I find I'm incredibly sensitive to preservatives and get a headache after as little as one glass of wine full of preservatives.

Like the laboratory text books there is no shortage of great wine making books. A huge number of them are written by people more qualified than us, with the relevant degrees and letters after their names.

We don't have them, we learnt everything by doing and trying and most certainly by reading many, many wonderful textbooks. And rather than reiterating what's in the textbooks, I'm showing you the behind the scenes parts of the winery. The parts they don't tell you about in the textbooks.

Here's an article I wrote about preservatives in wines many years ago.

Why do we need sulphur in a wine? – Sulphur in wines is used as an anti-oxidant and sterilising agent. It stops oxygen reacting with the wine and turning it into vinegar and kills off any organisms alive in the wine (including yeast in high enough concentrations). When a wine is produced under very clean conditions and stored properly, very little sulphites are required in the wine. With no sulphites whatsoever, a bottle of wine wouldn't last a year. Sulphites have been used in wines for thousands of years. The Romans used to burn chunks of sulphur to add sulphites to their wines and they've been used as common preservatives in foods since the 17th century.

What effect does sulphur (sulphites) have on people? – People sensitive to sulphites show asthma-like reactions, such as a stuffy nose, congestion, difficulty breathing etc. Some people will have no reaction to sulphites in foodstuffs while others will show a severe reaction. It's like any allergy: some people can die from a bee sting while others are just irritated by it. People with asthma are most at risk of a reaction to sulphites. Sulphites will be highest in young and sweet wines. After a few years in the bottle most of the sulphites will have gone.

Where does the Red Wine Headache (RWH) come from? – About 1% of the population is sensitive to sulphurs (sulphites) according to US Food and Drug Administration data and some people say this is the cause of headaches. Another group says the tannins in wines cause headaches. Tannins cause the release of serotonin (a neurotransmitter), which at high levels

55

in the blood can cause migraine-type headaches. But tea and chocolate can also have high levels of tannins and you don't hear of many people complaining of tea or chocolate headaches. But, some migraine sufferers are very sensitive to chocolate and tea and red wines. Yet another group of experts believe that the headache comes from the histamines in wine. People sensitive to histamines lack a certain enzyme and the theory is that this combined with the alcohol in the wine triggers the reaction and headache. The consolation of all this is that it's a natural part of wine that certain people can't tolerate and not any manmade additive. Some 'research' (cough, cough) has shown that common aspirin taken before drinking wines can slow or inhibit the onset of the RWH.

What's the difference between the headache now and the hangover the next day? – If you are sensitive to a particular wine, then you'll get a headache within about 15 minutes of drinking the wine. There are a number of causes for this as discussed above, but the key difference is the headache will show up very quickly. The 'axe in the front of the head' hangover the next morning is usually caused by dehydration and low blood sugar which is often the result of too much to drink. The best way to minimise the hangover is to eat while you're drinking and drink plenty of water. Moderation in the amount of wine you drink will also probably help.

Do white or red wines have more sulphites? – Whites! Regulations permit higher levels of sulphites in white wines than red wines and even higher levels in sweet wines. The sulphites are required in sweet wines to stop fermentation of the residual sugar in the wine.

Can I get a totally preservative free wine? – There is really no such thing. The fermentation process produces low levels of sulphites. These are naturally consumed as the wine ages and will dissipate quickly to the air once the wine is opened. There is the risk that wines with very low sulphite levels will ferment in the bottle and you'll end up with a fizzy bottle or worse still, vinegar. Dried fruits and other foodstuffs may have higher levels of sulphites than some wines.

And, the Australian Wine and Brandy Corporation states that on the label you have to include:

Any preservative, or in the case of P6, colouring or flavouring used in manufacture must be identified on the label by naming the additive type and the name of the additive or, the appropriate code of that additive eg. 'PRESERVATIVE SULPHUR DIOXIDE ADDED' or, 'PRESERVATIVE (220) ADDED'. No need to use capital letters.

Caution: Where there is no added sulphur dioxide, care must be taken in any claim that the wine is 'sulphur or preservative free', as sulphur dioxide can be produced by yeast. 'Preservative free' should only be claimed if there is <10mg/L of total sulphur dioxide in the wine.

The most common wine preservatives are 220 sulphur dioxide, 222 sodium bisulphite, 223 Sodium metabisulphite.

And, I wrote an ebook about storing wines. It was called the 10 most common wine storage problems and how to solve them. It's been ripped off and republished all over the interweb in the past years but I guess I have to take that as a compliment.

Labels

We lived through 3 distinct and different wine labels.

The first ones we inherited with the winery. And they were simply awful. This was before the ubiquitous computer generated graphics and peel off labels, but that's still no excuse, they were simply god-awful.

Next up we engaged a graphic artist, gave them pictures of the property and asked them to produce a graphic highlighting the views. This graphic was the background picture of our labels for the next 14 years. That's a very, very long time to keep one label alive and the return on investment was sensational.

The last change was to move away from our picture label to a simpler, more elegant label. We debated and argued back and forth about the new label and finally settled on a simple, all-text single label. No back label; all the information on one front label.

Lab Tests
When we started there were 2 choices.

You could do your own basic lab tests and have results in a few hours or you could send out your samples and have your results in a few weeks/months.

We chose the former and set up a pretty basic lab.

Today the technology for these tests is astounding. For not that many thousands of dollars you can get something that gives you an answer of too many decimal places in minutes. Kit priced at tens of thousands of dollars years ago now costs just a few thousand.

I'm going to get a lot of flak from this statement but making good wines is easy and there is no excuse for making bad wines. What is difficult and expensive is making great wines. Good wines start with great fruit followed by basic chemistry and common sense.

To make great wines everything must go right from day one. The fruit must be first class. The Grange makers pick the best fruit from within the best vineyards. The best botrytis wine makers pick the best berries from the best bunches from the best vines. The harvest temperatures have to be right so you don't oxidise anything from the vine to the winery. There's the new barrels, the right yeast, the right fermentation temperature and the gentle pressing along with controlled temperature maturation. In all, all these things and more come together to make great wines.

Just a few thousand dollars bought us all the testing equipment we needed to make great wines. The basic tests for alcohol, acid and malo were quick, easy and essential.

If you don't know where you are now, how can you possibly get to where you want to be?

There is no shortage of wine chemistry textbooks and there's over 700 new research papers hitting the ether every year. This means the basics of wine chemistry are very, very well covered.

So yes, a few basic tests put us on the way to making some great wines.

7 PROMOTING THE WINERY

Stall in the Corner

If you're reading this then I'm pretty sure you've got some serious interest in wines and winemaking.

Also, I'm sure you've seen a little winery stall tucked in the corner at just about every farmers market, festival, community event and whatever. There's a guy with grey hair or a couple with matching shirts, usually some flowers, a picture board with beautiful photos and a price list passionately presenting their wines.

But what does it feel like to do this day in, day out, weekend after weekend to thousands of people?

At first it's exciting. It's a nervous time when you're there early, everything's setup, the whites are chilled, the reds are breathing, you've tested each bottle in case it's corked and you're ready to go. All you need is the crowds surging through carrying off your precious bottles.

For every one pure wine enthusiast who genuinely wants to hear about your wines, you'll get 100 that are sticking their tasting glass out for another freebie. There'll be times when the day passes in a blur and you wonder what happened when it's pack up time. You've got a crate full of empty tasting bottles, you've sold everything you've brought with you, you've got a pocketful of cash and plenty of names for your newsletter.

There's other times when you've stood there all day checking your watch and wondering why 2 minutes seems like 2 hours. Your feet are sore, you're too cold, too hot, too dusty, too windy and plain too tired. You look around and there's an awful lot of unopened and unsold cases. The tasting bottles you opened a few hours ago are still half full and you've spent more time chatting with stall holder next door than any customers. It's cost you money to load up the truck, the table, tasting glasses, the credit card machine, get your cash register sorted, all your brochures, tablecloths, corkscrew, garbage bags and a trolley to move them all around. Then you'll take along a dozen or so cases of wines that you have to load into the truck as well. Now you've been standing there all day and sometimes you're heading home with $50 in your pocket.

Is it really worth it?

All that work to pack up, setup and tear down again. Is it really worth your time at this festival when you've got lawns to mow, grapes to look after, wines to check, people coming to cellar door and you've just spent the day out for a few lousy bottle sales?

Those are the days you'll find out if you really love what you're doing.

After a really crappy day can you pull off the welcome smile and go through your presentation for the hundredth time with the same enthusiasm and sincerity you had 10 hours earlier?

Well, if it's your winery and it's your name out there, you have to. You've got no choice but to grin, smile, go through it again and know you're building your reputation, you're selling your product and you're building your business 1 customer at a time.

Sincerity is the key and even a dog knows when you don't like it, so how much more so will your customers?

Me? I loved it.

From every 100 people who saw us as just a free drink, you'd find the handful of lovely people who became long-time supporters and loyal evangelists. These people kept coming back and back and supported us at all the festivals and events we went to.

It's these people that stick in your memory for a long time.

Wine and Cheese Days

You're probably wondering why I'm going through all the festivals, weddings and people side with so little on the wines and the vineyard.

Well, this was the reality of the winery.

After the first few vintages the grapes and wines become almost routine. Never quite routine, but you at least knew what you were doing. The real challenges come in selling the wines and getting your name out there. I'm not playing down the work or highs and lows of the wines and vines as they were there to look after and nurse every day of the year. However I spent more and more time on the commercial side of the winery the longer we were there. Part of that was our own success. The more people we got through, the larger we grew and obviously we spent more time in the cellar door and less out in the vines.

We started the wine and cheese days in 2003 to make something out of nothing. It was the same principle of MacDonald's serving breakfast. The building's there, the lights are on, the staff are in, so why not get some more customers?

We found that:

- Our visitor numbers were more than double on these weekends compared to other weekends
- Our average amount sold per customer went up
- We got a whole new range of customers who wouldn't normally turn off at a winery sign and more than 80% of them bought something
- Local advertising brought in another range of customers we would not have normally seen
- Customers enjoyed themselves more

After a few months of success we invited the other wineries in the road to join in and made it a 'St Helier Road Wineries' wine and cheese weekend.

We offered three Gippsland cheeses with several slices of crusty Italian style bread. The cheeses were cut up onto a dessert plate, covered with cling wrap and stored in the fridge. Bread was cut up fresh as needed and presented on a dessert plate.

We've tried serving a local olive oil with great results. It was served in a small white dish next to the cheeses.

We made the road signs (the first ones were pretty sad – but *they worked*), we advertised in the local newspaper and we promoted it through our own email newsletter. We even made our own wine and cheese signs to go on the road signs between the wineries in the street. Real road signs pointing towards each winery came a few years later.

We offered a hard, soft and blue cheese each time. Along with the olive oils they worked a treat.

We even had road signs 20km down the road to get people thinking about stopping in. The road signs went out the Saturday morning and we picked them up again Sunday evening. Rain, hail or shine, they went out and came back in every second weekend. The first signs were big sheets of plywood 8' tall and 4' wide (2400mm x 1200mm). Later we were more sensible and made rollup banners, but you've gotta start somewhere and start we did.

We did an absolute shit-load of work on this and promoted the hell out of it to make it work. It started as a small event but it grew to take on a life of its own. It ended up becoming an institution and people still say they see the signs every second weekend.

And, after 7 years of doing this it still worked and still brought in the crowds even during the middle of the coldest winter.

Community and Awards

Our biggest surprise came late in 2008 when we won the Bass Coast Shire Superpages Tourism Business of the Year and also overall Business of the Year awards.

The reason it was such a surprise was the competition we were up against. There were many much bigger and better financed ventures all through the shire. We were minnows in the big fish pond. But I guess we did something right.

We completed the submissions and lodged the paperwork and samples well ahead of time. It covered a lot of aspects about the business such as finances, business plans, management structures, product details and the 'shop front'. We were mystery shopped sometime during the process and I guess we got it right as the judges made special mention of the treatment they got.

Peter K went along to the awards night dressed in his standard issue wine stained t-shirt and jeans, what he always wears around the winery. He was busy promoting our wines at a table in the display section when we got called up. The hall was full of folks dressed to the nines: tuxedos, little black dresses, you name it. You can imagine him in his work clothes amongst VIPs. That was our style, we never made any apologies for it and again - it worked for us.

And then a year later we got the Agricultural Business of the Year award which was more than we ever could have hoped for.

These awards were a great note to go out on. I know it's a little trophy in the corner but it was a really, really nice validation that our work in the area was finally recognised.

And, during the peak of the drought the Gippsland region sent thousands of hay bales to the farmers doing it tough in Queensland. What little we cut from the back paddocks we offered up. At least we had some to send which was a more than many people at the time.

In the Press

Anybody in the public eye gathers attention.

Some of the articles we wrote and - as part of an advertising package - got them published. Others were real interviews.

A huge surprise was the cover of the Australian grape grower industry magazine. We hoped we'd get an article in, but we never dreamt we'd get the cover.

We were floored when it arrived in the mail. How does one small and unknown (at that stage) winery out in the country make the front page? That's usually reserved for the major industry players?

We thought it was Christmas when this came out.

And we've made the cover of other publications as well. The local council used our letterbox/roadsign on the ratepayers' booklets.

Yes, it was nice to have the recognition and the exposure sure helped us as well.

8 BOTTLING THE WINES

The Hard Way

We inherited the hardest, most bizarre way of bottling anything that I can think of. And what's even more amazing to me now is that in our dumbness we persevered with it for years. Ignorance, youth and lack of dollars lets you achieve a heck of a lot with very few resources.

We started with a gravity fed bottle filler. That means you put a header tank up high and a float valve on the bottle filler controls the fill level in each bottle. It's a beautiful and simple device that's been around since Adam was a child and worked well since then.

The only downside was the header tank.

The creations we concocted to put this tank up high make me laugh now but they worked. We stacked pallets, then we stacked potato bins (1100mm x 1100mm square timber boxes) and every combination in between. The white plastic tank came with the winery and these were utter crap. It's easy to criticise technology from 20+ years ago but even then they were crap. These things were made from sheets of Perspex glued together. After a while, exposed to the air and sun they started to un-glue with the obvious results. A first major expense was standardising on stainless steel tanks. No plastic, no junk, just nice industry standard stainless steel. They weren't cheap but they worked and they lasted and they'll probably outlast us.

Another huge change concerned wine bottles. Empty wine bottles arrived in loosely sealed pallets which we had to disinfect before they were used. Now they arrive on totally encased plastic-sealed clean pallets and all you do is cut 'em open and fill them.

Using recycled bottles is the other option that's disappeared. We used to buy recycled wine bottles, sterilise them and use them. 2 things happened to kill off this market in less than a few years. They were sticky, glossy, self-adhesive labels as opposed to traditional non-glossy paper labels and the influx of fancy shaped and coloured wine bottles.

The newfangled self-adhesive labels were much harder to remove from the bottle and this made the process not worth doing. Think about this. I can remember whenever you had a wine in an ice bucket you lost the label by the time you'd finished the bottle. When was the last time you had a label fall off in an ice bucket?

The other trend was new bottle shapes. As the wine market boomed in the 90's, the label designs and bottle presentation variety exploded. We went from a choice of brown or green riesling, burgundy or claret bottles to whatever shape, colour and weight you wanted. The recyclers picking up bottles outside restaurants now had 10 different bottle styles in each bin opposed to 3. The numbers apparently stopped working for them.

Each bottle had to be rinsed in an SMS or PMS solution, dried and then filled. So that was yet another manual handling step in the process.

Plus, they were all corked with a hand corker. This is fine for a few bottles but after a few thousand bottles your arms are about to drop off.

Electric corkers cost many, many thousands and these were lean financial times for us. The whole cork vs synthetic cork vs screw cap debate was heating up and sticking with old tech didn't seem like a wise investment. So we stuck with the hand corker and physio bills for many years.

The Easy Way

2 changes slashed our bottling times, effort and costs.

One was Peter Kozik building a fill level controller for the bottle filler and the other was going to screw caps.

Peter K is an electronics wiz-kid who, in his other life, has built RADAR and assorted control systems around the world. So a simple fill level sensor was a snack. It turned a pump on when the level got low and turned the pump off when the level was right. Pretty easy compared to stacking boxes and tanks close to the roof.

Now we left the tank on the ground next to our bottling line and worked wherever we wanted to. As you can see, our bottling line was pretty modest but, again, it worked and I didn't have to sell any body parts to finance it.

The other major change was going to screw caps. You've read all about corks and how wonderful they are in another section. For us, they were a royal pain in the arse. There is nothing in my opinion, I repeat nothing good to say about a natural cork seal for a good wine. Sure there's tradition saying this is how it should be done but tradition also states that we use leeches to cure headaches rather than high-tech aspirin.

A screw cap gives a perfect seal, it's clean, there's no possibility of TCA/cork taint and you don't need a corkscrew to open the bottle. And who hasn't had a corkscrew or your favourite Swiss army knife taken off you at an airport? No, there is no good, sound, repeatable, testable, believable reason to use a cork on a good wine.

The only reason the wine industry didn't move to screw caps sooner was simple market perception. A huge number of people still associate screw caps with a cheap wine and it's taken a long time to overturn that association. Even Penfolds trialled screw caps on Grange and have gone all screw cap for their premium ranges.

As you can see, we were quite passionate about screw caps. And the screw cap machine made life a breeze.

But back to corks for a minute. Before we went all screw cap we tried the popular cork alternatives, the synthetic corks. The first batch were too small and they fell out of the bottles. The replacement batch went in fine but you could break a corkscrew getting them out they were so damned tough. So we did what Goldilocks did and got something just right. We went to the highest possible cork grade money could buy and stayed with it. It was the only acceptable cork grade for fine wines until we went all screw cap.

Filtering

I've lost count of the filters we used.

We had filters so fine they could take the colour out of wine. We used cartridge filters, bag filters and plate filters. Each had a place and a time and they worked.

And we had a pretty reasonable range of pumps as well.

The real buzz was seeing sparkling clean wine streaming into a tank. No picture can do it justice and there's no way I can pass on the beautiful smell of wine wafting up.

It was another of the 'wow' moments in the winery.

End Result

Another great thing about screw caps was not standing them upright for 24 hours after filling. With a cork, the bottle must stand upright for a day so the cork expands and grips the bottle.

But you can lay screw caps down straight away so it saves the double handling.

I know it doesn't sound like much, but just have a think about how much time it takes to pick up, move and lay down several thousand bottles? Anything we could do to cut out unnecessary, un-quality-adding work we grabbed with both hands. So this was a gift for us.

9 FANCY PORT CROCKS AND BOTTLES

Australiana

Tourism was a huge part of our business. We were off the main road on the way to the Penguin Parade at Phillip Island and on any day we'd have up to hundreds of people coming through. China, Singapore, Thailand, Hong Kong and Korea were part of our core business.

We were in the wine business.

No, I take that back.

We started out in the wine business and then realised we were in the tourism business. We made wines and we sold to tourists. And as a side note, I've lost track of how many people wanted to see our wine 'factory' and then we had to explain it's a winery, not a factory.

But sometimes people didn't want a 'normal' bottle of wine; they wanted something a little fancier.

We created many wildly different and fancy port crocks to fill with our luscious fortified wines. We did 3 Australian themed crocks: a penguin, a koala and a map of Australia, each with their own story.

The koala bottle had an interesting past you'd never guess. It started life as a, believe it or not, lamp shade sometime in the 50s or 60s. Someone made it into a port crock and soon enough every potter in the country had their version of it. It worked for us and we sold thousands of them. Some of them had terrific detail while some came from moulds that'd been used too many times and had very little detail.

They held around 700ml of port and we used a natural cork in them. Our first step with a new batch was to wash and drain them. All the crocks were glazed inside but who knows what they went through during shipping.

Next was to find some snug fitting corks. The variance in bore was astounding. We broke some corks trying to drive them into the crock while others flapped around. The difference in sizing was amazing. But we had to get a good seal for a top product, otherwise they'd leak in someone's luggage and we'd be in all sorts of strife. The last step was to wax seal the top. We had the cork in but the crock was going to spend its life sitting upright which meant the cork would be dry, not wet. The wax gave it an airtight seal so the port would last for years and be a great drink when opened.

It was a lot of work.

The wax came from our trusty wine supply place and the wax heater came from the beauticians' supplies warehouse. Yes, it's the same wax heater the beauticians use to heat wax to wax legs, etc.

The Australia shaped bottle was bright blue and some had a flag on the front, some were unadorned, some had 'Australia' across the front; we tried it all.

There were even different sizes of this, some as small as 500ml while the largest we had was over 1L. And they all sold. We paid the money, we had the moulds made and commissioned various potteries to supply us. Unfortunately they all followed the same pattern. The first deliveries were a great quality product which unfortunately got worse the longer we dealt with them. Sad but true.

The last Australiana port crock was the penguin. The winery was on the way to the Penguin Parade at Phillip Island. According to which Government department statistics you believe, it was the 3rd most visited attraction in Australia.

The Opera House was number 1, the Great Barrier Reef was number 2 and the little penguins were number 3.

We actively pursued a lot of tourist buses and it was great business for us.

We started with our own penguin mould. I found a wildlife sculptor who made us a penguin sculpture that was 'mould' friendly. By that I mean something that stood upright, was stable, held about 600-700ml of port and could easily be made into a 3 or 4 part mould.

Then we had the physical moulds made, including masters. 'Masters' were the moulds from which the production moulds are made from and I can go on about this for hours but I'll spare you this time around.

After some more money going out the door we had our first production Penguin Port Crock complete with "The Gurdies Winery" decals.

And they sold like warm beer at a Pommie soccer match.

The final version of the Penguin was a smaller and more petite design from a local potter. He had the moulds ready to go so we used his.

And again, they sold like hotcakes.

All these port crocks were incredibly labour intensive to organise, clean, fill, seal and store. We provided cardboard boxes and then bubble wrapped each individual one for each customer.

Regardless of how much work it was, thousands of port crocks later I still get a kick out of seeing them.

Custom Port Crocks

After seeing our fancy port crocks people started asking if we'd do custom designs and eventually we said yes to our regular customers.

Some of the designs were easy and straightforward. Others involved scores of different designs and sending many samples back to our customer.

Were they worth doing?

Well, yes and no.

In terms of income I'd say no, since it was a lot time for us to arrange the production.

In terms of exposure, getting the name out there, flow on orders, return trade and other good things, I'll say that everything we did to get the winery name out there was worth it. And it comes back to diversifying the business and income base. I believe it's better to have one hundred ways to bring in $1, rather than one way to bring in $100. It spreads the risk.

And, the port crocks looked absolutely stunning with a gold print.

Fancy Glassware

The people walking in through the door came from all points of the globe. Some just wanted a souvenir with Australia written on it. If it had wine in it, then all the better.

One of our regular suppliers stocked bottles they'd originally aimed at the cosmetics market. We adapted the male and female torso bottles to ports and muscats and did a roaring trade. The liquid volume was very small, around 400ml, which was great for us as our ports and muscats lasted longer. It took a lot of time and effort to wash, fill, cork, wax and tag each batch. We bubble-wrapped each one for every customer as well.

The other bottles?

Yup, it took time and effort to create these but they all sold and sold consistently.

We had one that's got a bunch of grapes inside the bottle which started life as an olive oil and vinegar bottle. We used a pale muscat on the outside and a red port for the bunch of grapes inside. For a while we couldn't get these fast enough. Whatever we put out on the shelves would go that week.

Then the quality of the bottles started changing. The glass got thinner and weaker. Some arrived broken and we started breaking some just by pushing in the corks. After reports started trickling back from our customers of bottles broken in transit we stopped this bottle. Someone somewhere decided to save a few cents by making the glass a little thinner resulting in the destruction of an entire product line.

And that was a shame as so many people loved these bottles.

What was fascinating about all these fancy bottles was the sales cycle or rate. Some days we'd have the shelves emptied of one particular bottle. And then we'd go a week until we sold another one of that particular bottle.

There was no rhyme, reason or pattern. It was not people from one particular country of origin buying one particular bottle.

Nothing.

No rhyme or reason.

We logged every customer walking into the place, how they found us and what they bought. I can assure you there was no pattern to the sales as I spent hours poring over the records looking for one.

Port Bottles

Our standard bread and butter port bottle changed many times. Over time we went from 375ml up to 500ml and down to 400ml and so on with many changes in shape.

We'd be happily buying pallets and pallets of one particular port bottle when the supplier announced they could no longer 'source' this bottle.

So we'd get fresh sample bottles, test them, find corks for them, later we'd get new screw cap designs, change the label sizes, get new artwork, print new labels and tags and off we'd go with a fresh design.

It was a hassle to change, it was a cost to change.

The first time we were forced to change we worried that people would stop buying our ports as we'd (gasp – horror) changed the bottle.

But the bottles simply kept on selling.

Why we worried so much about it the first time I'll never know.

Stock Port Crocks

We collected a fair few stock port crock bottles. Different potters across Australia produced different crocks and we ordered many 'stock' product lines.

A little gas bottles really appealed to some people's sense of humour. I've lost count of how many ended up as gifts for someone who was "always running out of gas for the BBQ". And they did look great but what a bastard to wax the tops. The cork was below the level of the guard so we had to fill a cup with hot wax, dip the corks and do it quickly before the wax set.

What seemed really strange was how poorly the golf ball port crock sold. We thought we'd be knocked over in the rush by all the golf-mad people out there. Luckily we didn't have the house mortgaged on this product as sales were at best a trickle out the door.

The bunch of grapes bottle has a slightly different story. We had the moulds made for this crock from scratch.

In my next life I'm coming back as a mould maker just to collect the salary these folks do. I swear they all have a different Ferrari for each day of the week. The phrase "we had the moulds made" rolls off the tongue so easily now. To be fair to you I'll cover the process in a little more detail.

First we had a 'bunch of grapes shape' made. So we had a sculptor produce this for us and this took a few attempts and more than a few weeks.

Next, we go to our regular mould maker. It takes a few more weeks to get him to look at it and fit it in his work schedule. The moulds shrink as they dry so he has to estimate the bore of the neck so the corks will seal. It gets better: different size moulds shrink by different amounts. And you can't force-dry a mould as it will distort so they're air dried which takes another month.

Now we take the moulds to the potter and get a dozen samples done. Yet another few weeks pass.

Some look like crap while we can't keep our hands off the rest. We use these to test the corks, match the wax colour, print the tags and test how we pack them for sale. And we use these to design the decal for future releases. This takes a few more weeks to get artwork done, decals made and shipped to our potter.

And that is how you get a port crock made.

The port crocks all sold well.

We tried different colours, different tags, different decals and different whatever we could test.

And they all sold well.

Trams and Trains

One of our potters was also a closet sculptor. He had access to the mould makers and he was wonderfully creative.

He's now a retired potter but we had the privilege to work with this man and share his products.

The winery was 93km from the heart of Melbourne, Australia. Melbourne has one of the last remaining tramway networks in Australia. So having a tram port crock seemed like low-hanging fruit to the tourist market.

We modelled it on a W class tram. They're still in service in Melbourne and you can see them clanging down the streets every day. After factoring in the cost of the custom-made timber display cases, the decals and the work going into such a detailed crock, it wasn't a cheap bottle. But we still sold lots and lots of them.

And the steam train, the real train has long gone to the museum but what a port crock that was.

They looked great and they sold well. The only criticism was that the train crock held 1.5L of port which made it too heavy for most folk to carry back overseas. Even that didn't deter the train 'nuts' who bought these.

They Got Away

We were doing so well with the fancy glass bottles that I looked further afield and tracked down a supplier in Germany with some amazing glass.

Visiting them I found the quality of their glass so far ahead of what we were getting in Australia it left me in tears. And it wasn't just the quality; it was the variety they had.

They had a sailing boat bottle, a pair of luscious lips, a raging bull and even a stiletto shoe. I was like a kid in the candy store.

I've still got the few samples I came back with carefully tucked away.

Unfortunately we never shipped in any pallets from these folks. Other business got too busy...

10 BIG WINE BOTTLES

This may be a little off-topic with the winery however, it was a key part of our business. The margins on a bottle of wine plummeted over the last 10 years as the larger wine companies produced more and more wines and dumped them into the markets.

All the fancy bottles, port crocks and now the latest innovation of big wine bottles had fantastic margins. Instead of a $25 bottle, we now had a $500 bottle. A little bigger than usual, sure, but still a wine bottle with fantastic margin on it. There's no shortage of guides and books on running a winery which include a lot on the finances. We're sharing with you what the real side of it was like: not the textbook, not the pretty brochure, but the good, the bad and the ugly.

The big wine bottles started when I saw some mind-boggling glass engraving on a crystal sports trophy. I wondered why we couldn't put this onto a wine bottle, and why not a big wine bottle at that?

The answer was of course we could. It took me a very long time to figure out how to do this, but we eventually got it right.

Step one was finding the big wine bottles. Now they're pretty common. 10 years ago they were rare beasts. We tracked down the suppliers and bought what they had. The common sizes we used were 1.5L, 3L, 6L, 9L and 18L.

And, we even wrote a history of big wine bottles and where the names came from.

Customers had 2 ways of buying a big wine bottle. One was to get a standard, off the shelf engraved bottle saying the standard things like "Happy Birthday", "I Love You", "Happy Fathers Day" and so on. The other was to get your own artwork done complete with custom back label.

This is where it got more complicated and more costly. We had a range of standard layouts that worked well and satisfied most people. We'd draft the artwork, email it back to the customer and work with them until they were happy. It was a considerable investment for the customer so we wanted it to be right. Especially when the bottle was going halfway around the world: it **had** to be right.

The technology was quite simple in theory but hard in practice. We used a graphics design package, CorelDraw in this case to do the artwork. We'd either use a standard design or work off the customers' artwork.

Some people were great to work with while others we were glad to see the end of. But that's just one of the facts of working with the public. Ask anyone in hospitality or a customer facing job and you'll get the same response. Some days you're the dog while other days you're the fire hydrant.

Back to the process.

CorelDraw did the artwork and then we would cut a vinyl template using a sign making vinyl cutter. Then we'd 'pick out' the vinyl template and stick it to the bottle. The rest of the bottle was masked with tape and paper to keep it clean and scratch free.

Next it was into the sandblaster to 'cut' the design into the bottle. There was a very fine line between not deep enough and too deep and destroying the vinyl mask. When you got it wrong it meant you'd just ruined a bottle. When you got it right it was quick and easy.

After that we'd strip off the mask and clean the bottle. This meant cleaning off the sticky muck from the mask as well as the dust and grit from the sand blast. Sometimes it took half an hour to clean the muck off. And if we didn't clean it out then the colour wouldn't take.

Now we coloured the cut parts. We used a super-rare antique furniture colouring paste to fill in the glass. We experimented with all sorts of colours and methods but it quickly came down to customers wanting 90% gold and 10% silver using one particular brand of product. The fancy colours never really caught on.

Putting in the colour was messy and fiddly. You forced it into the cuts with a stiff bristle brush, wiped off the excess and polished the bottle. But the colour worked its way into every tiny imperfection, scratch and nick on the bottle. This meant more cleaning during the polishing stage which could take anywhere up to an hour.

Now the bottle was ready to fill. We'd wash and sterilise each bottle, fill it, gas it and cork it. The corks on the larger bottles were up to 30mm diameter. Do you have any idea how much force it takes to get a 30mm cork into a bottle? My hands still ache at the thought.

Once the cork was in we'd sit the bottle upright overnight. This let the cork expand and seal properly.

Now we'd wax the top of the bottle. The idea behind the wax was to give an airtight seal. Obviously the big bottles would spend most of their life standing upright. That meant the cork would dry out (this is the main reason you lay down bottles in your cellar – to keep the cork wet) and let air in to ruin your wine. The wax sealed the bottle.

Now a 9L bottle weighs about 12kg. You've got to be very gentle and yet very quick when waxing them. You must dip the neck in the hot wax just enough to cover it, keep it there for some 20 seconds, lift it out, turn it so there's no drips or runs and then plunge it in ice water to give it a glossy finish. 12kg doesn't sound like much but after you've done it a few times 12kg gets real heavy, very quickly.

The final step was a back label.

Our idea of treating the back label as a greeting card worked a treat. We'd create a big bottle for a wedding and print up the back label on a sticky A4 size sheet. During the event or function everyone signed the back label and stuck it onto the bottle. Do you think anyone would ever throw this out?

We got an order for a bottle for the Prime minister of Australia, John Howard. And we also got an order for the then boss of Ford Motor Company Australia, Geoff Polities, so they were pretty popular.

My favourite big wine bottle story centres about an 18L bottle. That's 2 dozen normal sized wine bottles in 1 single bottle. A fellow ordered one with a standard front label and bare minimum details on the back. After a while chatting with him it turns out he wanted the bottle as a centrepiece for his new wine cellar.

So far so good.

He was moving house as he'd outgrown his current 4,000 bottle wine cellar. Yes, that's right, four thousand bottles and he had outgrown that. And the new house had his 13,000 bottle wine cellar. There were times in the early days, before a major bottling run where we, the winery, had fewer than 13,000 finished bottles in stock. And this was one private cellar.

Our wine lover absolutely loved his big wine bottle when it was off loaded from the truck…

We had custom display and shipping cases made for each bottle size. These required kiln dried, export safe timbers as so many of our bottles went overseas. We'd bubble-wrap and pack up the bottles tight as can be before they shipped. And in all the years we only ever had one break in transit and I'm pretty happy with those numbers.

And we even made custom side labels for most of the bottle shipping cases.

The big wine bottles were a lot of work and time and they looked absolutely fantastic when they went out.

11 PLANTING NEW VINES

Ask ten experts how to best plant vines and you'll get ten different answers.

We learnt early on to ask everyone and then make our own decisions on what worked for our site and this is just what we did with our new plantings.

We knew most of the vineyard work would be done by machine so we laid out the plantings to suit. 'Deep ripping' means running a tractor or dozer with a huge hook on the back down the middle of each vine row to open and loosen up the soil. Each vine row was deep ripped to give the little vines the best possible start in life and we power-harrowed (levelled) the block to make it tractor friendly. We also sowed a cover crop to keep the soil in place and put in machine harvester friendly posts.

The machine harvester works by shaking the fruit off the stalk. I talk more about this in the machine harvesting section but these harvester friendly posts were steel posts that flexed as the harvester moved past them so all the fruit was picked right up to each post. A nice big thick pine post had no flex in it so the harvester missed about 30cm of grapes each side of a non-flexy post. And this meant hand picking around the posts which kind of defeats the purpose of machine harvesting.

A question we got all the time was how much does it cost to plant an acre of grapes?

The list below shows approximate prices to plant one acre of grapes. That's 15 rows, 90m in length, 3m apart and a vine every 2m. I know I'm mixing acres and hectares, but some measurements are common in the industry and everyone's comfortable with the mix so I'll stick to it.

Prices are approximate and they're here to give you an idea of what's needed. I've also included what time of the year to do each task. This example assumes we'd be planting the vines in spring so we started work on this block the year before. And, we're in the southern hemisphere so summer is over Christmas time and June/July is the middle of winter.

- Order and pay for grape vines, phylloxera resistant grafted rootstock vines - $2,363 - November
- Soil test to determine what's missing from the soil - $250 - December
- Spread lime, gypsum and other soil requirements—it would be rare in Australia that lime and gypsum wouldn't needed as we have very old acidic soils and vines need a neutral soil pH - $800 – January
- Plan and peg out the layout of the vineyard, best done with the help of a surveyor but two people, some common sense and time will do just as well - $1,350 - January
- Deep rip the land for root penetration and drainage, you need a BIG machine to do this and you have to rip to a depth around 500mm (no haulage fee included) - $600 - February
- Sow cover crop to preserve the soil structure, build up soil organic matter and nitrogen content - $150 - May
- Turn in cover crop to incorporate organic matter - $90 - September
- Power harrow land to level area and seed permanent grass sward (grass in the vine alleys) so the soil doesn't

blow away and you can work in the vines during wet times - $195 - September

- Buy treated pine posts for end box assemblies, posts around 175mm diameter are required as a fully laden trellis gets very heavy - $2,400 - September
- Buy steel posts for each row, one is required every 6m – the steel posts flex in the ground and the harvester can pick around them, pine posts in the middle of the row don't flex and the harvester will miss the grapes 300mm each side of the post or break the post - $1,260 - September
- Buy wire, 1 irrigation wire, 1 fruit wire and 4 foliage wires for each row, foliage wires can be added later, but it's easier to get everything done at one time - $695 - September
- Buy vine guards, these work as a hot house around each vine, they protect against rabbits, wind and chemical spray drift - $1,013 - September
- Buy irrigation pipe, drippers, connectors and assume we are connecting to an existing irrigation system so no pumps or filters are included in this price - $1,200 - September
- Contractor to drive treated pine and steel posts into the ground - $1,200 - October
- Contractor to build end assemblies - $400 - October
- Put wires up and strain as required - $450 - October
- Install irrigation lines, drippers and connect to existing irrigation system - $450 - October
- Weed spray in vine row to leave green grass in the alley ways and the new vine is planted in bare earth so there's no competition from weeds for nutrients and water - $210 - October

- Plant grape vines—this can be back breaking work, each vine is dug in and watered as you go - $300 - November
- Tie vine up to the fruit wire—we want to have the vine up to the fruit wire as quickly as possible so it can start providing fruit and we want nice straight trunks on the vines so it's easy to work around them - $300 - November
- Put on vine guards - $300 - November
- Slash down the vine rows, a regular task during spring to autumn, required on average every two weeks - $90 - November
- Buy & spread fertiliser—organic fertiliser to give the vine a kick start, apply about 1 ton to the acre - $830 - November
- Weed spray in vine row, a regular task that can be helped by mulching under the vines, without the weed spray the young vine is competing against the weeds for nutrients and water - $210 - December
- Slash down the vine rows, ideally this is with a side throw mower so the cut matter provides a mulch under the vines - $90 - December
- De-sucker vines—the vine will try to grow shoots from each bud on the trunk, we have to open the vine guard, snap off these suckers and clip the vine guard back on and this has to be done regularly during the growing season - $300 - December

Total for the first year for 1 acre - $17,495

The figures above were done more than 10 years ago so you can easily double them. The tasks remain the same but I doubt you'd find anyone working for the hourly rates we had 10 years ago.

I based these times and figures on some new riesling vines.

Two guys had this block laid out in one and a half days. That's starting from a bare paddock and finishing up with all posts and vines marked out and ready to go. There was a lot of walking and cross checking and more walking but we got it done. I'm sure a surveyor could've done it faster, but we worked with what we had and it worked.

Ready to Go

We had our posts in and the wires were up. The irrigation was still to go in but otherwise we were set to go.

We killed off the grass with a weed spray to get rid of weed competition for the new plantings. A few weeds will suck an incredible lot of water and nutrients from the soil and we found by keeping the weeds away from the young vines we saved a year in setup times. Yes, it was that much.

We found it easier to sow a permanent cover grass before the posts and wires went in. Other vineyards sowed down the alleyway only and some places just kept whatever pastures were in place. We found it quicker and easier to sow everything and then weed spray the undervine row.

Planting the Vines

We planted this block with cuttings from our existing riesling block. We did this by taking cuttings during winter and propagating, or 'striking' them in sand filled boxes over winter. Then towards the end of spring we planted them out.

Striking the cuttings is one of the 'black arts' things you see in the agriculture world and my mind still boggles as to who originally came up with this method and why?.

Let me describe the process.

You take cuttings about the length of your forearm. Then you tie them in bundles of around 40 cuttings and plant them upside down into sand. That's natural coarse river sand and yes, they go in upside down. Come next spring when you wash them out you'll find tiny hair-like roots. Don't ask me why this works, it just does. I've seen it over and over again. Plant them the right way up and you get fewer roots, if any. Plant them upside down and you get plenty of roots.

We got a lot of people coming up and asking for cuttings to put a few grape vines in their backyard. I remember what it felt like when we were first starting out and the internet was close to non-existent compared to what it is now and knowledge was pretty thin on the ground. So every time someone came up to ask for cuttings for their 'backyard' vines, I'd describe what to do and watch their eyes promptly glaze over. But, the people who followed this advice got their vines in the ground the following spring. Those who didn't got lots of little dead sticks in the ground and they'd start all over again and hopefully do it right this time around.

We were blessed with beautiful black sandy topsoil and this made planting super easy. It was as easy as sticking a shovel in the ground, rocking it side to side to make a hole, dropping our rootling in and covering it over again.

Each vine went directly under a dripper and we watered it in the day it was planted. A question many people asked was how much water do you need? The answer is obviously: enough. The way to find out how much is so simple in hindsight it beggars belief that anyone would even ask but I'm saying that having worked with vines for 18 years. You walk around with a shovel and stick it in the ground a few times. If the soil is moist down in the root zone then you've got enough water. More water going deeper than the root zone is just wasting water. Why would you water if the vine can't use it? Why? So much of the vineyard was bare arsed common sense and people complicated it for the sake of complicating it to make themselves look good or sell you something.

Sure, if you've got 2,000 acres of vines in the ground then you'll need moisture probes as walking around with a shovel would be a fulltime job. But we were small and it worked a treat for us.

Our strike rate on this patch was sensational. We only lost about 2 vines in the entire patch the first year which was an outstanding strike rate. Unfortunately the following year we brought in a vineyard manager and lost about 20% of these vines.

We eventually threw him out after just one too many cock ups and licked our wounds (and wallets) for several seasons afterwards.

Putting on the Vine Guards

We were expanding our vineyards at the peak of the Australian winery boom so every man and his dog was in the market flogging the latest and greatest snake oil product imaginable.

There were a dozen different types of vine guards for the taking simply by browsing the latest grapegrower magazine. There were tall ones, short ones, single use ones, tubes, boxes, staked ones, tie down ones and even multi coloured ones.

We settled on a corrugated waxed cardboard guard we could clip to the wire, was easy to open, easy to reseal and we could use over and over again.

The vine guards were a personal little hot house for each vine. They kept the rabbits away, they shielded each vine from the all important weed sprays and it kept the wind off the fragile new leaves.

The only downside was maintenance. The weeds loved the little hothouses as much as the vines and the weed sprays couldn't get in there, so several times a season we had to weed the new vines by hand. That meant opening each guard, pulling out the weeds, cleaning out the snails, getting rid of suckers on the vine and closing up the guard. It's easy the first few times, but after the first thousand vines your knees start complaining and you know you'll be seeing vine guards in your sleep.

Some people tried old milk cartons, some tried soft drink bottles cut open at both ends and some tried no guards whatsoever. Everything worked to some extent and everyone had their opinions based on their own results. This is what we did and these are the results we got and they worked well for us.

12 VINE BUDS AND SHOOTS

19th September, give or take 10 days is budburst anywhere in Australia. That's the date when average soil temperatures climb above 10C and the vines claw back to life.

After the long winter filled with dark bare vines the first spots of green are a feast for sore eyes as there's some colour in the vineyard at last.

The chardonnay and Pinot Noir are first to show their buds while the shiraz and cabernet sauvignon were always last.

The green leaf came back in a shock of green. Every vine sticks out a small leaf checking if it's safe to come out after winter. One day there are a few stray green flashes and then next day there's some more and then in what seems like overnight it's all green.

The vineyard showed apical dominance on some vines. Apical dominance describes the growth pattern where the buds/shoots grow faster at the cordon ends and slower near the crown. It evened out by the time we had 20cm shoots so I never worried about it. It looks odd but that's the way it was and it always grew out a few weeks later. The text books say it's caused by nutrient deficiencies. All our petiole and soil tests showed the levels were fine. Go figure…

When we were late to finish pruning (which was most years I'm ashamed to say) the vines started dripping water from the fresh pruning cuts. As the temperature rose the vines came back to life and started circulating their sap. On a warm spring day we'd see droplets raining down from fresh cut canes. This gives you some idea of how efficient vines are. There's not many other plants out there that'll match a vine's growth rate. No harm done with this water dripping from the vines as it was no more than nature at work.

At this stage we were keeping an eye on snails and that's about all. And as long as the weeds were sprayed the snails weren't a problem. Rather than worrying about synthetic chemicals to kill snails it was easier and cleaner and greener to take away their breeding ground in the weeds around the vine base. No breeding ground equals no snails. There's a lot to be said for watching nature and her cycles and then acting on them.

We'd mulched and swept under the vines so the place was clean and at this stage of the season there wasn't enough leaf to worry about spraying just yet.

First Shoots of Spring

The vines were growing like crazy. Given a warm sunny day and plenty of water we'd see 1-2cm growth a day. The rows were bright green, the vineyard looked magnificent and it was the first time I could see how well (or how woefully) we'd pruned.

After the first few leaves sprouted, the flowers formed. The time from flowering till capfall, which is when the flower starts to fill out into a bunch of tiny little grapes, was a nervous time. Any powdery mildew infection or even too much wind damaged the delicate flowers. As soon as the flowers were damaged, you've lost some crop without even really starting the season.

Powdery mildew was the most harmful at this stage and it was a 'perfect storm' situation as it thrived in the moist humid spring days. As soon as it hit the flowers I knew it'd cause damage. Even a mild infection could damage say 15% of the flower and this meant 15% crop loss before we'd harvested a single berry. It was heartbreaking to see this happen and more so when we had a run of days I couldn't spray.

No words I can give here describe the loss and frustration at seeing this happen. All the work and planning and cost and hopes and dreams dry up from one little mildew sucking away at your livelihood.

And then you get a spectacular day with the sun shining through the new green growth, the fresh air, the water views, you make a great sale at the cellar door and suddenly the world seems pretty good. It comes back to learning and accepting the patience that farming brings you, having the time and resources to act when needed, and simply savouring the amazing beauty Mother Nature rolls out for you every single day.

First Fruit

Somewhere when you've turned your back for a week or so the flowers filled out to become round green berries. And this is the first time you can see the varietal bunch shapes.

Pinot noir, riesling and chardonnay have small tight bunches.

Shiraz is long and open with a classic ice cream cone shape.

Cabernet sauvignon has large bunches not as open as shiraz.

And each variety comes with its own challenges.

Pinot noir, riesling and chardonnay are extraordinarily sensitive to botrytis. We had to get our botrytis sprays spot on to coat all the berries before the bunch closed up. When I missed that window we got hit with botrytis. What I mean by the bunch 'closing up' is just what it sounds like. The shiraz and cab sav had open bunches like you see in table grapes. The riesling and pinot and chardonnay bunches closed up tight with no space between each individual grape.

Hot weather saved us most years as the heat stopped the botrytis spores spreading. And when the worst happened and they had spread, the heat dried the infected berries and stopped the rest of the bunch rotting.

13 COVERING THE VINES WITH BIRD PROOF NETTING

The Gurdies covers lots of native bushland and plenty of open grazing land dotted with large healthy gum trees. There are plenty of creeks running through the place and every paddock has a dam or two. In other words it's a birdlife paradise.

The glossy vineyard and winemaker magazines advertised all sorts of fancy bird scarers. We had a pick from noise cannons, hawk outline kites, radar controlled noise generators and sparkly wavy figures. And I'm sure these are all wonderful and effective bird control methods when you're protecting thousands of acres. However, our grape holding was like the Wild West Cavalry's fort sitting all alone, smack bang in the middle of hostile territory. We were a tiny outpost in the middle of the wilderness.

Wine grapes aren't normally on your average bird's dietary wish list but as the weather got drier and drier, more of the birds natural food sources dried up, burrowed deeper or crawled away. So their next best food source was us: the supermarket in the wilderness. The drier it got the more desperately they sought my luscious, sweet, sugary grape and veraison signalled the full scale assault.

Any vine row left uncovered was stripped bare by the end of the day. If it got to the stage where we saw the birds showing interest in the vines we knew we'd left it too late and the crop was gone.

Once the nets were on we had a daily cycle of checking the nets morning and evening and this was a helluva lot of work. It meant hours of walking and pulling nets so the vines were covered right down to the ground. Any gap was as open invitation to them.

Cliché alert: If I hadn't seen this happen with my own eyes I wouldn't have believed it.

We'd see the birds walking on the ground next to the nets trying to lift the net with their heads. Sooner or later they'd succeed and then merrily feast away. They knew, **they knew** how to get under the nets.

Our last and most successful netting method covered two rows at a time. This means the net spanned two rows and draped vertically down the outside of each row. I'm sure the birds could see and smell the grape through the nets. They'd hang in the nets along the outside row bouncing in and out till they finally snagged a berry through the net. They'd swallow this and move onto the next bunch.

The smallest rip or tear was like a velvet rope outside a nightclub announcing this was the place to be. They'd swoop in and feast away till it was time to go and then out they'd fly.

I'm sure I've forgotten countless other bird 'stories' but these give you an idea of what we faced.

We used a variety of machines, frames and methods to cover the vines and I cover those in the coming sections.

The one part of the operation shared by all methods and machines was that we needed 3 people. One person drove the tractor while another 2 worked either side pulling the net out and over each vine row.

We quickly figured out you couldn't wear anything with buttons as this snagged the net real quick. After a few hours of tugging at nets our hands and fingers were crying uncle and you were covered in crap raining down from the net above you. Sticks, twigs and anything else got in your eyes and hair and stuck to anything you had on. As the stuff rains down on you it goes down your shirt and all the biting bugs go with it so by the end of the day you've covered in bites. Plus you're netting in the heat of summer so you're sweating that hard your shirt's stuck to you and you feel the sweat running down your back and into the crack of your arse. And the smallest stick or left over pruning tangled the net instantly. The lightest breeze caught the nets and turned them to sails, making whoever had the upwind side curse and swear and work that much harder.

Even with the latest hydraulically spooled net machine it was still a physically hard and manual task.

It was tough for the driver as well. You were turning constantly to look back at the net, you listened for either of your people calling a stop to fix a tangle, you kept the tractor going straight, you matched your ground speed to the net going out and you stopped as soon as the net tangled on the net machine. It was multitasking at its finest.

Throw in the frustration factor of nets catching seemingly everything and tangling and I hope you can see why for us, netting was pretty high on the least favourite list of tasks in the vineyard.

Covered Vines

The nets formed a sea of white sails spread over the vines.

They look so serene and peaceful and soft.

If only they could speak of the battles we shared to put 'em there.

One of the dumbest bits of advice we ever fell for came from a 'highly qualified' consultant. He was on staff with a vineyard supply company and part of dealing with them was use of their 'free' consultant. Unfortunately as per the iron clad rule in life, you get what you pay for, and we paid dearly for his 'free' advice.

This fella recommended a new method where we clip the nets together to form one continuous blanket. This saved on nets as there was no drop down each second vine row. Over one or two rows this was no big saving. However when you're buying nets by the kilometre the savings were attractive.

This turned into an unmitigated disaster costing us tens of thousands of dollars.

We should have clicked that this would not end well after we'd spent hours and hours clipping the nets together. We used thousands of plastic clips supplied by the same company to join the nets. And you're now working under the nets to clip them together overhead. You try holding your arms over your head for the next 10 hours and you tell me how tired your arms get?

Pretty much straight away the problems started.

Some birds will get into the net by some means at some time. That's just a fact borne from close to 20 years of observation. I'm sure if we bought nets made from bullet proof Kevlar and concreted them in place, I'd come back the next day to find at least one winged creature inside.

Covering 2 rows with 1 net made it easy to get the birds out. Just lift one end, walk along and shoo the birds out.

Now when you've got several acres under one continuous net, how the bugger do you get all the birds out? Some vine blocks looked like an aviary and we lost a hell of a lot of grape to the birds. We had to open up one entire end of the net and then find a dozen people to walk down each row yelling and clapping and making noise to empty the nets. This was not something we could do every day as you just can't find a dozen people every day at a time to suit you.

But that wasn't the worst of it.

The wind load over a few acres of net was tremendous. The tipping point for us was finding half the vine block uncovered after some fierce winds. All the work to cover them was undone in 15 minutes flat.

We spent the next day re-laying the nets, but the damage was done. Just a few short hours without cover was all the birds needed to strip the rows bare.

We fought the suppliers for months over our losses but nothing came of it. There was nothing in writing and we got all the usual excuses of qualified advice and trying to pin the blame back on us saying we hadn't laid the nets down properly etc. It ain't rocket science or brain surgery. We were simply laying out big white nets.

Needless to say we have never dealt with them again.

Other Net Machines

We evolved through several different types of net and net machines.

First off was a god awful plastic black net covering one row at a time. Think of recycled plastic drink bottles and you've got the consistency of this material. The edges were razor sharp and they were hard to see on the ground or on the vine or pretty much anywhere else.

They were stored wrapped on cardboard tubes about 1,500mm long in one of the old sheds. The rats, mice, snakes and assorted critters had a field day with the cardboard tubes during the off season.

We put them out via a mast on the carry-all behind the tractor. One driver and two poor bastards stretched this black blanket over each individual row. As the net was around 3m wide when stretched it didn't quite reach the ground on both sides. So we were stapling and wiring the bottom sides together under each vine row. This was ugly back breaking work. Letting them drape on each side left the vines open and let the birds fly in and help themselves.

It was incredibly labour intensive.

The tractor mounted hydraulic roller worked from the end of the row as it had to be at right angles to the net. This was before all the high-tech winery gizmos boom many years later. So the net had to come off the vines and lay on the ground. As you can imagine this picked up every leaf, twig, pruning and stick it possibly could. Two people then had to fold the net neatly in half so it came off the roller and draped on the vines in an orderly manner next season. And on top of this the person on the tractor working the hydraulics would juggle the controls so the net came in nice and slow and didn't slice up the net 'handlers' with its razor sharp edges.

This net came with the winery and we persevered for a few years before moving on. The high-tech gizmo era hadn't yet arrived so most things were still pretty low tech and 'agricultural'.

Next up we moved to the new technology woven nets. They were white and covered two or even three rows at a time. This was long before the tractor mounted hydraulic drive net machinery came onto the market.

We welded up an aluminium mast with what's best described as a basketball hoop at the top and mounted it to the back of the tractor. We built this from scratch on the property and it worked fine. We tried a steel version but the weight of this made it too hard to handle, hence the move to aluminium.

The new woven nets shipped in 300m lengths. Our row lengths varied from 80m up to around 120m so we cut nets to suit each row length and stored them up on shelves in numbered wool bale bags. It was hard work moving the bags and then stacking them back, but it worked. And every crawly critter under the sun loved our net bags nicely tucked away each season. I'm sure I've been bitten by a fair percentage of every biting insect or bug on the Australian mainland. I can tell you what bug is what just from the bite and I've even built up immunity to some bites. For instance, bull ant bites don't swell up like the used to. I'm pretty sure the bull ants haven't got any friendlier so it must be the immunity after many bites.

For the next revision of the manual net machine we moved the mast to the front of the tractor. This was much easier to work with as the driver wasn't looking back all the time. The downside was a lack of power steering on the tractor. With all the weight out front it was a real hassle to drive. It was super easy to work with and visibility was brilliant, but it proved too hard to drive.

Now you get quad bikes with power steering so the idea of having a tractor without power steering and air-conditioning and sequential gearboxes seems to be stone age, but that's what we had when we started. The manual net machines worked fine and we netted a lot of vines over many years.

The first hydraulic powered net machine came to us via a contractor. In the end this contractor was an utter disaster but that's another story. He had a Credon Netwizz machine spooling the nets onto a giant spool. We could fit a 300m net onto one spool. It was easier and quicker but you still needed three people and storing away these monster spools was now a two man task. Pulling in nets was a revelation. Before we pulled them in by hand, now the machine pulled them in and wound them up while we guided the nets.

For the final update to our net laying machinery we bought our own hydraulic net machine. We found it takes a while to learn to 'drive' any machinery and for us it took two seasons to master the ins and outs of our net machine. The exposed nuts, bolts and sharp edges were surely one of the most bizarre things about this machine. You're working with nets that stick, cling and catch on the nearest object, any object that is. And here's a machine that's chock a block full with bolts and sharp edges? We had it wrapped in duct tape by the end of the first day and, while this helped, there were still parts of the design we never did figure out.

The neighbours knew straight away when we were netting and the neighbours were a fair way away.

How could they tell?

By the yelling and swearing wafting across the normally tranquil countryside. It was still a lot of physical work to net the vines.

Damage to the Nets – Storm Damage

At times it felt like Mother Nature was having a bad day and I'd just cut her off in traffic so I was getting the full nine yards of her wrath.

Right up there with the strangest things I've seen was a willy willy (think whirlwind or small tornado) plucking one single net from the middle of a block. The wind threw the net over the power lines and draped it over the front house. The power company people were wide eyed and laughed out loud when they arrived to untangle our net from their transformer.

We rolled it up and put it out again and just kept going. What else can you do?

The regular strong winds lifted the nets and pushed them off the vines and that's why we had our morning and evening net checks.

Taking Off The Nets

Taking off the nets was either a walk in the park or a pain in the arse.

Any wind made this hard work. But, when we decided to harvest we had no choice but to pull in the nets that day. Waiting for the perfect sunny day wasn't an option, we had to go with what we had when we had it. Pulling in the nets was the same as putting them out. You needed three people and plenty of patience.

The beautiful glossy brochures and demo videos showed the nets quickly and effortlessly lifting off the vines while spooling smoothly onto the spindles.

However…

They'd tangle around the machine itself and you had to climb onto the tractor cab to pull them out.

They got torn during the growing season and you stopped and waited and fixed the holes.

The vines kept growing while the nets were out. We were in a cold climate wine region so we had a very long ripening period. The warmer parts of Australia had finished vintage in February while some years we hadn't even netted the vines in February. So after a few months more growth we'd be ripping the nets off the vines where the canes had grown through. By finished vintage I mean all the grape is picked and in the winery. The winemaking continues for many more weeks and months and years, but all the grape is off the vines.

And by far the worst task was picking sticks and canes out of the nets. Every small stick, every leftover pruning, all the summer prunings and anything else we hadn't mulched to buggery stuck in the nets. We'd be pulling them out at the same time we were guiding the net off the vine.

Do you have any idea how tangled a cane gets in a woven net?

It all comes back to time and preparation and getting things 100% right before doing the next step.

We seemed to race against the season each year and were never 100% on top of things before we had to act. This came from juggling too many things at a time and trying to do too much with too little.

Anyway, we got some great vintages and lifetime memories and I've had the privilege of working with some of the finest people I've met in my life. And it's funny how you get to see a person's true colours when the going gets tough.

The last task was to tuck away the nets for another year.

As we rolled up each net we'd dump them near the vine row where we drove out. They looked like giant marshmallows dotted around the vineyard.

Sometimes it was 2 to 3 weeks before we could get back to them. Then you'd stack 3-4 nets in the trailer and haul them down to the sheds to stack away. It'd take 2 people the best part of a day to stack away the nets. They're heavy, they're an odd shape, they tangle with anything that even looks their way and it's always great when we're finished for another year.

14 MATURE WINE GRAPES

I want to say it again: you must be obsessed with wines to make great wines.

You can not try to make great wines. You either make great wines or you make not-so-great wines.

Like Yoda said in Star Wars: **"Do... or do not. There is no try."**

The magic moments in the winery were so good that the blood, sweat and tears fade from memory and your spirit soars.

Seeing full, mature grape bunches is one of those times.

We've pruned the vine, we've babied it through the winds and diseases during the growing season, we've mown the alleyways and sprayed weeds under the vines, we've put the shoots up on the trellis, we've netted the vineyard and now you finally see the fruit.

The beautifully shaped full bunches of rich fruit hiding behind the leaves by the thousands. You walk up the rows sampling the berries and the sickly sugar sweet syrup fades to leave a clean acid aftertaste. There is nothing, nothing like seeing and tasting the mature fruit on the vine.

Words help paint the picture but words don't give you the sight, the smell, the grass underfoot and even the sound in the vineyard. If you don't passionately love what you're doing, then you'll never make a great winemaker. Anyone who says they're making wines as a job and hasn't the will to go the extra 10 miles and nurse the wines through the night will never make great wines.

It's easy to make sound, good wines. There's plenty of technology to help you and it's really not that hard.

The difference between good and great is a vast gulf.

The difference between good and great is the passion, resources and commitment to making it work that comes only when you ARE passionate and committed to making it work.

If you can't see the magic hiding in the vineyard, then you'll never get to see the magic in the bottle.

If you can't see the magic, then follow some other passion as life is too short to waste in a job that makes it hard to get outta bed in the morning.

Just Sprayed Grapes

All the mature grape pictures have little white specks on the grape. That's copper-sulphur mix coating the fruit and leaves. We sprayed this 'damn close to organic' mix to coat the vine rather than using synthetic systemic chemicals. This layer of 'muck' over the vine 'stopped' the mildews and moulds. The synthetic systemic chemicals 'fixed' the problem.

It was cleaner and greener to stop the problem than having to fix the problem.

The Leaves are Dying

This one stumped me the first season.

All through the vineyard the leaves closest the cordon died off as the fruit matured. I instantly did what any good viticulturist does and panicked.

What had I done wrong?

What had I sprayed?

Had my pruning killed the leaves?

Were my vines dying from some exotic and unknown disease?

The answer was much simpler than any fanciful scenario my mind could ever conjure.

A vine leaf lives about 100-130 days and that's it. Do the math and you'll find that the end of September until January is roughly that many days. And only the basal leaves (the ones closest the cordon) were dying as they were the first leaves to form.

The leaves further up the cane formed up to 60 days later as the canes grew and sprouted leaves.

It makes sense when you think about it and add in a little vine knowledge.

Plenty of Leaf

When the canes grew and the leaves sprouted, the vineyard turned to a sea of green.

The drier years showed up the vine leaves as the only green for miles. Grass underfoot turned to yellow straw while the gum trees stayed their typical drab greens.

The wetter years turned up the dial on the green-o-meter. Bright green grass carpeted the alleyways and the extra water buffed the vine leaves to a brilliant green gloss.

And we often had canes draped on the ground - it's me running late with my shoot positioning. They should be trimmed and tucked away by this time but some years we dumb ran out of time.

Spiders Alive

Look closely at any clean and green vineyard and you'll see spider webs wrapping the grapes.

Some people will scream in horror at the mere thought of spiders near their future glass of wine. But the truth is the exact opposite.

Having the tiny little spiders surviving and thriving was the kiss of God for the vineyard. They're a most reassuring sign that all's alive and well and green and clean. A vineyard with no little bugs is a barren wasteland with no life and usually full of poisons. Unless you're living in a high rise apartment you'll see bugs and insects and flying critters all the time. Can you imagine how much fly spray it'd take to get your home completely bug free?

Lots and lots I'm sure.

Now imagine how much pesticide it'd take to keep acres and acres of vineyards totally bug free?

Is this really what you want to be drinking?

Testing the Fruit

We tested sugars and yields coming up to vintage as they were the key things we were interested in.

We tested the sugars with a refractometer. There are other ways to do it, but a quick walk through the vineyard with a handheld, temperature compensated refractometer gave us all the information we wanted.

And the testing was easy.

Just a few drops of juice squeezed onto the slide showed an instant Brix reading.

The refractometer measured Brix. The Brix scale is named after a German scientist, A F W Brix. It measures the density of a liquid. Brix can be measured using a hydrometer or a refractometer. A hydrometer is calibrated with a sugar solution: 0 degrees Brix is pure water and 20% sugar solution is 20 degrees Brix. When we test the berries for ripeness we are testing for the percentage (density) of soluble solids (sugars) in the juice.

So when I'd say we have about 24 Brix in the shiraz, I know we've got about 24% sugar. This gave us close to 13% alcohol in the finished wine. Not quite a 2:1 ratio but close enough for a field evaluation.

It was a quick and easy way to test for sugar levels.

The volume or yield testing wasn't quite so simple. It took a lot of time to do accurately but once you did it right the first time, each season took only a few hours to update. I'm sure there are other methods out there but this worked for us.

The best way to show the work involved is to work through some of my results. For this example I'm looking at a small chardonnay patch.

First I've got to find out how many bunches of grapes I've got on each vine. So I'll walk along each row and from a sheet of random numbers I'll stop at every 2nd, 3rd, 4th, 5th or 6th vine and count the number of bunches.

In this example I get (taking a small sample) 20.18 bunches per vine. This being the average of 11, 15, 13, 24, 32, 32, 24, 15, 13, 13, 14, 17, 16, 24, 28, 32.

Next I take another random sample of how many berries per bunch. You walk up and down the row and when you get to your next random vine, stick your hand out, without looking, and count the berries on the first bunch you touch. At this point you hope there are no snakes up in the vines.

In this example I get 55.75 with this being the average of 81, 45, 56, 71, 70, 40, 67, 54, 56, 55, 46, 53, 62, 44, 40, 52.

From these same bunches grab a single berry and get an average weight. I get 2.4g here.

In this block I have only 16 rows with 45 vines in each row. So when I do the math, I end up with 1.81 tonnes of grape.

The only thing that'll change as the berries grow is the weight of the berry. I don't have to re-sample everything else, so once that work's done I'm good to go.

It probably doesn't sound like a whole lot of work but we had 12 separate blocks of vines. So yield estimates took quite some time.

Ripe Grape Problems - Sunburnt berries

On top of the crawling bugs, flying bugs, slithering pests, mildews, moulds, birds and every other creepy crawly out there looking for a free feed, you have to look after the sunburn.

Unfortunately there's not much you can do to control this; it's something else sent to test your patience.

A particular weather pattern during summer hit our crop hard. A day of rain followed by a very hot day sunburned and then split open our berries.

We had about 15mm of rain one day followed by a 36C day the next. All the westward facing berries looked like split open peas.

The grapevine's a very, very efficient water pump. It soaked up the rain, pumped it into the berries and swelled them up. The hot weather the next day split them apart.

Fortunately this happened early in the season and the following hot dry weather shrivelled the split berries. If we'd had wet and cold weather, the bunch rot would've wiped out the rest of the bunch.

Botrytis

Here's a brief history of botrytis wines I wrote many years ago;

When we tell people we make a sweet white wine, the first question we get is: "Is this a botrytis wine?" So let's see exactly what is a botrytis wine?

Botrytis bunch rot or grey mould is a disease that exists in all vineyards worldwide and is caused by the fungus botrytis cinerea. Botrytis can hit grapes at any time but the most common infection time is when they're very nearly ripe. Botrytis bunch rot stays alive during winter on the bark, in dormant buds and in debris under the vine, which is just another reason to keep the vineyard clean. Botrytis spores are produced in spring and infect leaves and berries. Water's needed for germination and long periods of wetness with high levels of humidity give ideal spore production conditions.

An infection period during spring kills off the flowers and/or the berries on the vine. This means a vastly reduced yield.

Instead of the full number of ripe berries on the bunch we may be getting only 50%. Any break in the skin of the berry from birds, wind, hail or sunburn provides an easy infection entry point. Eventually the entire bunch becomes a grey mouldy mass of spores. In dry weather the berries dry up and there's very little damage further on. During wet weather the berries burst and spread the mould further.

We manage botrytis in the vineyard in two ways: environmentally and chemically.

Environmental management includes vine canopy changes to maximise the airflow and decrease humidity. We used a VSP open trellis, pruning and leaf plucking in summer to manage the canopy density. Everything possible to minimise berry splitting. We go to great lengths to keep the weeds down under the vines and the ground as clean as possible as botrytis can survive on vine prunings and even weeds.

Chemical management involves sprays to kill the fungus before it multiplies rapidly or 'blooms'. Wet humid weather is the danger time when we have to monitor the vineyard daily and spray regularly. Flowering and 'bunch closure' (when the bunch rapidly fills in, late spring to early summer) are the two crucial periods.

Legend has it that in 1650 a priest had his harvest delayed when the Turks attacked. When they returned to the harvest they found a fungus had grown on some bunches. They wondered what the wine made from these grapes would taste like and were pleasantly surprised. The Germans and then the French were next to follow with the botrytis or 'noble rot' wines. The best grapes for noble rot wines are riesling, gewürztraminer, semillon, sauvignon blanc and chenin blanc.

The botrytis fungus will puncture the skin and slowly draw out the moisture from the grape. This produces grapes with much less liquid than normally ripe grapes and consequently a much higher sugar concentration. Grapes are carefully harvested. The harvest may occur in stages with one pass picking only the ripest grapes. You then wait for a few days and harvest again to pick up only the very ripest grapes in the block. If you leave it too late you can smell the vinegar walking through the vineyard. Then you know you've left it too late. You have to pick the grapes while they're still moist raisins, not when they've dried up.

Needless to say this is a very slow and precise process. You definitely can't machine harvest a botrytis crop. The very rot that you are fighting off for most of the year is what you desperately hope for in the final weeks and days of harvest.

The term 'late pick' is used synonymously with botrytis wines but is not the same thing. Late pick means just that. The fruit is left on the vine to ripen very slowly and wither on the vine. The same concentration of sugars that happens with 'noble rot' happens naturally in late pick grapes. The botrytis infection just helps speed up this natural process. The harvest is delayed while the grapes literally wither on the vine, producing raisin like fruit with incredible sugars and favours.

If all the sugar in these grapes were fermented we would get a wine of around 20% alcohol content. However, the yeasts used to start the winemaking process die when the alcohol content reaches around 15%. This leaves a beautifully balanced wine with good crisp acids, plenty of sugar for sweetness and lots of alcohol. An environment of approximately 15% alcohol content by volume becomes toxic to the yeasts. Normally the yeasts would happily continue multiplying and consuming sugars until they ran out of food but in the case of botrytis wines the yeasts do their job so well that they produce a toxic environment for themselves.

In the winery the grapes are hard to work with. The juice flows like molasses, not like normal grape juice. The pumps are working harder and everything is sticky. The botrytis grapes are always the last ones to be picked so they're coming through when the winery has been cleaned up after harvest so they're almost an afterthought.

But when you open a sweet bottle of 'noble rot' wine, all the troubles are truly worth it.

And, an interesting point. In Australia it is illegal to add sugar to wines. We can add acids (tartaric, citric etc) but not sugars. In the rest of the world it's the other way around. You're permitted by law to add sugars (chaptalisation is the winemakers' term for sweetening wines by adding sugar) but you're not allowed to add acids.

If you weren't a total cynic, you'd put this down to a bureaucratic translation bungle a hundred years ago – but let's not go there.

Hen and chicken

'Hen and chicken' is the fruit disorder where the same bunch will have some normal sized berries and little green unripe ones scattered in. It usually shows a mineral deficiency such as boron, zinc or molybdenum.

We did regular soil and leaf tests in the first ten years. But after that you could pretty much pick what was happening by walking around. And rather than waiting for something to go wrong, we simply added the trace elements and minerals into our regular sprays. It was easier to prevent problems than having to rush around fixing them.

15 HARVEST TIME

Picking by Hand

The accepted 'wisdom' said that hand picked fruit gave better quality wines.

We only dealt with facts. If we couldn't measure something then it wasn't worth doing. Why would you do something that you couldn't measure?

We found no difference in final wine quality between hand picked and machine picked fruit.

None.

None whatsoever.

Not a cracker.

We had the advantage of different varieties ripening at different times. So we didn't have to bring in 40 tons of fruit on the one day. We could spread it out over several weeks.

Why did we pick by hand and also by machine? We found the closed bunch varieties like pinot noir and riesling didn't pick well by machine. You had to beat them hard to get them off the vine and this broke open the berries so we lost a lot of juice. These varieties we picked by hand.

For the more robust varieties such as shiraz and cabernet sauvignon it was pure logistics that pushed us to machine harvest. The high yields meant that getting all the fruit off in one day required an army of pickers or one machine. That's why.

The single biggest hassle in the early days was finding enough pickers. Family and friends came for the first vintage and then most, not all, had something else to do and I can't blame them.

One year we tried a local school with disastrous results. The deal was we'd pay X dollars per ton of fruit picked. I can't remember what X was, but we made it worth their while.

The problems started on the day when the pickers arrived with every other member of their extended family.

The picture of a pre-schooler sitting on a pile of my nets working feverishly to cut through as much as she could with a pair of cutters still haunts me to this day.

Eventually we got the harvest in. We paid them for their efforts and then noticed just about every pair of cutters we'd loaned out had gone home with our pickers.

Such is life...

Next on the list we worked to recruit a group of locals. This worked well but once we'd trained our people, the other wineries around us poached them for their harvests. That was the problem. Every winery in the immediate area had harvest at close to the same time we did. It was a mix of mums, local farmers and some retired folks. And do you know who made the best pickers?

The local little old ladies, that's who.

They were the quickest with their hands, they enjoyed the day out and I guess the pay helped. Who would have guessed?

But even they got tired of the work so the last model we used was a contract labour company. We advised what day we needed a dozen people and they arrived on the agreed morning.

For us it was easy. They brought their own lunch, cutters, everything. We got one invoice for the day and they were quick. That was just another part of us growing up from a small family winery to a commercial operation.

The work for us started early and finished late. I've covered some details in other discussions here, but I'll go through it again so you can appreciate the work involved with each harvest.

We had one day to bring in one varietal, say the chardonnay. We'd be out early that morning putting out the foam boxes for the pickers. If we didn't have enough people to bring in the nets that day, we'd leave the nets on the vines as the pickers lifted each bit of net as they worked down the row.

Two pickers worked face to face down the row. You'd think there's not much to miss in the grapes right in front of your nose but you miss a lot on your own. Your partner on the other side of the vine picks up the bunches you miss, plus you've got someone to talk to as it gets pretty boring.

We kept a good supply of water and Band-Aids close by. Your hands and cutters got sticky real quick. A short rinse was enough to get rid of the sticky grape juice. As for the Band-Aids, no matter how many times you've picked grapes and how 'cut proof' the secateurs' design, you'll still slice open a finger every so often. Luckily they were all small nicks but they still draw blood and you've gotta keep it clean.

Our pickers dropped the bunches into the foam boxes and as the foam boxes filled up the pickers pushed them under the vines. The vines shaded the boxes from the sun and let us drive up and down the vine row with the quad bike and trailer picking them up. Invariably the pickers left the boxes sticking out just far enough that I'd have to stop, get off, push the box under the vine, drive a little further, stop to pick up the box and repeat this down the vine row. This went on all afternoon until the hundreds of boxes were safely tucked away in the cool room.

Picking by Machine

Time was always our enemy. We were working our day jobs and running the winery weekends and evenings and any other spare minute we had.

After one particularly long and dismal weekend with very few hand pickers and bad weather close by, we looked around for a small machine harvester and found one being demonstrated not far away. We went to see it working and convinced them to bring it to our property for another demo.

When it arrived we found our tractor wouldn't run it so we borrowed one for the day. The fellow from a winery up the road helped us out. I'm sure we've repaid the favour many times over in the past years, but there's no dollar value you can put on help like that.

There's an old saying that you see people's true colours when dealing with money and adversity. I've yet to see this wisdom proven wrong and we found out very quickly who the real people were and who was along for only the good times.

Our 2WD tractor had no creeper gear (super low range giving a ground speed of between 400 and 1,500m/hr) and low range was still too fast. It needed a creeper gear otherwise it didn't pick cleanly. So we bought a new tractor to run the new harvester which made it one of the more expensive years we'd been there.

The fellow who sold us the harvester was Italian in the true sense of the word. Full of the spirit of life, talked with his hands and always had a story to tell. After the day harvesting he and his mechanic stayed the night with us. We talked and drank and laughed and joked till way early in the morning and it was one of those nights that sticks in your mind forever. I can't recall how many bottles we went through but that was one of the dangers of dinner parties at the winery: I could never use the excuse that we'd run out of wines.

Our Volentieri mechanical wine grape harvester was spot-on for our place as it was easy to operate, turned in a very tight area and didn't need huge horsepower. 10m clearance at the headlands at the end of the vine row was the magic number to turn the harvester. With the older plantings we moved posts and fences and whatever was needed to get the magic 10m clearance. New plantings were much easier: we mapped out a 10m turn zone at the headlands and kept enough space all round the block for easy tractor access anywhere.

You can see it working on a slope in some of the pictures. Not that we had any steep slopes, just easy gentle inclines. Each wheel was adjustable up or down by several feet, keeping the harvester square to the vines. This was all electric over hydraulic control.

The harvester was simple in principle but a real bastard in execution and use. The tractor needed a standard 540rpm PTO (Power Take Off) and two hydraulic remotes. One remote had to be full flow while the other could be full flow or on demand. The full flow remote controlled the harvester boom, self tracking, wheel height and swing in. The non full flow remote controlled the side shift drawbar. The hydraulic oil flow volume was not huge and it happily ran off our 45hp tractor.

The electric controls ran off a 12V DC connection back to the tractor. The controls were mounted on the ROPS next to the operator and controlled the: boom, door on the chute, left wheel lift/drop, right wheel lift/drop, override for the auto-track and the side shift drawbar.

Two huge noisy fans above the fruit conveyors sucked out any leaf, stalk or cane while it was still in the body of the harvester and kept the MOG (Material Other than Grape) or leaf, stalks, sticks etc low. The fans made a deep booming sound and when the harvester hit a resonant note you could hear it a kilometre away.

We needed three people to run it. One person drove the tractor, one drove the chase bin and one person rode up top to supervise and pick out the larger sticks.

The harvester works by shaking the fruit off the vine so maintenance was continuous and horrendous. When something failed during harvest, everything stopped. The one and only time it failed totally we had to call in the pickers the next day as we managed to fix all other breaks on the day. And even that could have been avoided if we'd stuck to the plan and not taken shortcuts. The one and only time we'd taken a shortcut, it came and bit us on the arse.

We desperately wanted to finish 4 lousy rows but were running short of people and it was already dark. We started picking with no one sitting up top to watch out for sticks, canes etc. And yes, the first thing we got was a piece of broken vine big enough to strip all the paddles off the top conveyor. So we had no grapes, no harvester and another bill for several thousand dollars of damage. All because we didn't follow our own rules and tried to rush it.

One day we'll learn…

The harvester had another 'feature' that took us a while to figure out. If the chains and belts were not tight, it'd jam at random times. So I'd stop the tractor, jump off and pull one of the belts by hand to get it turning backwards. Starting up again might be enough to keep it running for the rest of the day or sometimes 2 minutes. We never figured out the exact cause and never figured out how long it'd keep running in between glitches. But when it worked it really worked a treat.

Over the years we updated and changed the beaters to bow rods, replaced the elevator buckets, the conveyor fingers, the top conveyor paddles and even the sides of the harvester with massive stainless steel sheets. Not to mention welds on the shaker mechanism and new bushes, bearings, etc. In the end it was a little like granddads axe that's had two new heads and four handles but it's still granddad's axe.

16 PRUNING 10,000 VINES

Hand Pruning

You can split hand pruning into three types:

- Cane pruning
- Spur pruning
- Clean up spur pruning after a machine pre-prune

Cane pruning

Whenever the topic came up in conversation about owning a winery I could SEE the mental image forming in the other person's mind: I'm sitting on the verandah, surveying the vines rolling across the foreground while supping a glass of my finest vintage.

The times we could sit back and relax were pretty few and far in between. There's no other way to put it - the vineyard and winery were a lot of hard work. It was a magic lifestyle and the sights, sounds, smells and experiences are with me for a lifetime but it was still a – lot – of – hard – work.

Pruning, cane pruning in particular, is as far from this 'sitting on the porch' image as you'll ever get. You're standing in the winter wind and rain, cutting and pulling canes on each vine.

There's plenty of textbooks on pruning, but let me describe the process to cane prune one vine.

First you stand back and look at the vine. In my mind I'm pruning two years out. As a side note, we cane pruned every 4-5 years and spur pruned in between. 'Conventional' wisdom says you get better quality fruit by cane pruning every year, but we never, not once, had any evidence to support this. The crops were some 10-20% lighter on a cane prune as you just can't get the same bud numbers, but the quality stayed the same regardless of cane or spur pruning. But back to the story. I'm looking at what the vine will look like two years out. What it'll look like when I've established my main cordon and I've got first year shoots coming up. That's the first step and that's something that simply takes time and experience to see.

Next, you take the big cuts on each cordon. The cordon is the main horizontal arm on each vine so when you put down a fresh cane, it stays a cane until the first shoots come off it and then it becomes a cordon. Yeah it takes a while to figure out the right words to use. We worked on a VSP trellis (Vertical Shoot Positioning meaning all the canes are pushed under trellis wires to keep them bolt upright) so there were only two cordons. We tried Scott Henry trellis with disastrous results but that's another story. I'd use my big hand loppers, or the chainsaw, to cut each cordon and on the more vigorous growing varieties I'd take another two to three cuts on each cordon so it was easier to pull out.

I'd pull out the cut cordons and have another look at the vine. From the fresh canes I'd select the best ones and lay one down on each side. I'm using what's called a fibre vine tie to tie the cane to the wire: that's a fibre coated tiny bit of wire that lasts about one season and then rots and rusts away. With the fresh cane laid down and tied down, only then would I go back and cut off the other canes. I've lost count of how many times I'd snap a cane while laying it down. And when I'd already cut off the rest of my new canes, I'd be stuck. So I'd only ever cut the other canes after I'd laid down my new, next year's cordon. At this stage I'm using my pneumatic secateurs. We did some pruning with hand secateurs but that novelty wore off very, very quickly and the pneumatic ones came out real quick.

Last I'd clean up the ends where the new canes overlap the adjoining vine. I'd leave no more than one hand width overlap. I'd also clean up any suckers on the trunk while I'm there and put the fruit wires up to the start of season position.

You have to do this for every vine on the property. You stand in front of every single vine on the property and prune it back to two fresh canes.

On a good day I could cane prune 3-4 rows per day. And that's going at it pretty hard. When you've got 160+ rows to go it's a long, cold, wet, mind numbing slog to get through this.

Spur Pruning

Spur pruning leaves the cordon intact while taking off the current year's shoots and growth so it's easier and quicker than a cane prune. I still have to 'touch' each vine on the property but I'm doing a lot of small cuts and no major ones. There were times when I'd see a cordon that really needed replacing so I'd cut that off and lay down a fresh cane and that was a part of the continuous improvement on everything you saw or touched or came near. I was always looking with the 'owner's eyes'. The 'owner's eyes' means you never walk past a cigarette butt in the car park, you stop and pull out the single new weed that's come up in the garden overnight, you straighten up the stock on the shelves when you're walking past. It's a continuous process, not something you do every once in a while and not something you turn off and on when it suits you.

The spur prune process is similar to the cane prune and I followed these steps.

Step one again was to stop and look at the vine. What I was after was the textbook result of a beautiful 2-bud per spur vine. The reality was always a compromise. The aim was to work towards how close could I make the vine in front of me look like the textbook picture.

Then you start cutting. I wanted 2 buds per spur. So the first cut is 2 buds away from the cordon. Depending on the variety of vine I would make several more cuts on the same cane so it was easier to drag it out. shiraz and cab sav have a very tangled growth and it was very hard to pull the cane out in one go. So with the pneumatic cutters I'd make two, three or even more cuts to pull out the short lengths.

The last steps were to clean up the suckers at the base of the vine and lift the foliage wires to their start of season position.

And that is pretty much a spur prune. You're still out there in the cold and you're still touching every vine and you're still getting scratched from the canes. We would typically cut 6-7 rows per day per person so it was quicker than a full cane prune.

Clean Up Spur Pruning After a Machine Pre-prune

To speed up the pruning process we contracted in a barrel-pruner (a type of tractor mounted mechanical pruner) to run a pre-prune. Some years we treated the pre-prune as the final prune but that depended very much on the skill of the pruner operator.

In the pre-prune years we had the barrel pruner come through and cut approx 20cm above the fruit wire. Then it was a simple matter of walking along with the pneumatic cutters and taking each spur back to two buds. The barrel pruner also shredded the canes into 10cm long pieces so there was very little pulling out left.

The barrel pruner didn't cut right up to the posts so we cleaned up those areas by hand.

To put it into perspective: we could prune 7-10 rows per day which is a huge timesaver over a cane prune and even a spur prune.

And I'll say it again, we had no evidence of better or worse crop quality of cane prune over spur prune. The reasons we cane pruned every 4-5 years included:

- Keeping the buds close to the cordon. After each spur prune, the base buds got further and further away from the cordon. By year 5 we had buds starting some 15cm from the cordon.

- Give the vines a rest. The crop loads following a cane prune are up to 20% down on a spur prune. The vine doesn't have to work as hard to ripen as many berries so it gets a chance to lay down additional carbohydrates for the next season.

- Replace missing spurs. Some buds died, some got damaged during harvest, some got ripped out, etc. We lost canes and spurs and they needed replacing and a cane prune restored the bud counts and got the cropping rate back up where it should be.

- Hygiene. Some diseases build up and over-winter on the cordons. Phomopsis, botrytis and downy mildew were the main ones we worried about. By getting rid of the cordons, we cut down the disease pressure. For the first few years we dragged the prunings out of the vine row and burnt them. However there was no evidence of more of less disease pressure by burning the prunings or mulching them. The emphasis here is evidence. If we didn't see the results, we wouldn't do it regardless of what all the wise men said. No result, no action.

Machine Pruning

We eventually trialled a full machine prune with great results. And this worked very well mainly because we found a very good operator. This fellow could control his pruner to give an accurate average 2 buds per spur.

Sure, it wasn't perfect.

Sure, it left some canes around the posts.

Sure, we still had to lift the wires.

But all the vineyard was pruned in one day and we got very good results the following vintage.

It would have been nice to have this machine in our shed rather than calling in a contractor. But it cost some $55k so it was a little hard to justify this expense for 6 hours of work a year.

The downside was the next pruning season. The vineyard looked very 'furry' especially around the poles where the pruner couldn't reach. It was more pruning work to clean up after the additional growth but the fruit quality was still there.

So the summary I draw over the years is to say that (for us) the method of pruning had no measurable effect on crop quality.

Summer Pruning

We used a VSP trellis system. We also tried Scott Henry but could never get it to work so we stuck with the cool climate industry standard VSP. Even with all the cane tucking and shoot positioning, some shoots dropped out or grew out. And, we had vigour issues with the older vines. They were planted too close together so they grew like crazy and gave us 6m long canes some years. We spaced the new plantings further out so the vine was working harder and producing more fruit and less cane. That worked on the new plantings, but we couldn't really uproot a 25 year old vine and move it 400mm to the right.

The summer prune was a run along the vine row with a hedger to cut the canes sticking out. And we did this by hand. So you're walking along with a petrol powered hedge trimmer cutting the vines. Yes, it was hard work and yes, it killed your arms. And yes there are tractor mounted hedgers to do this but they were out of our budget for something that we didn't do every year.

The summer prune did two things. It let more sunlight and air onto the bunches which helped ripening and cut down diseases. Second, it let the nets drape easily over the vine rows. If the vines were bushy then we'd run out of net before it got to the ground and, as you saw in the netting discussion, any opening will let some birds in.

The cut ends on the canes and the vine row looking neat and clean – that was a treat to see.

Leaf Plucking

We tried this for a few seasons with no real results. And like I've said before, if we couldn't measure the results then we didn't do it.

Some places swear by it, but we could not find any benefits.

Replacing a Trunk

The oldest vines were planted in 1982. So after 25 years some needed a pretty radical pruning. The crowns had grown above the fruit wire, they were huge and they had to go.

We took two approaches to replace the crowns, depending on the vine.

One approach was to pick up a sucker just below the crown to give us two fresh cordons. This was the easiest and quickest as we had two fresh canes in the same year and no loss of productivity. But it depended very much on each individual vine and if we had suitable suckers. Once we chainsawed off the crown, we were back to clean fresh canes straightaway.

The second approach took two seasons to implement and we used it when we had no suckers just below the crown. When pruning we picked a sucker from the base of the vine and tied it to the fruit wire. In the second year pruning we took off the old trunk just above last year's new sucker and put down fresh canes from this sucker.

We painted an anti-bacterial paint on the big cuts is. We tried all types of antibacterial paints, sprays etc. We even tried thick black tar based roofing paint and guess what?

They all worked.

I could find no difference between the $100 pruning specific anti-bacterial wonder potions and a tin of $20 black roofing paint. As long as we put something onto the cut we had no problems.

But when we left the big cuts untreated, we had problems.

This caused some eutypa dieback. To fix this we cut back until we hit fresh wood and then treated that cut with antibacterial paint. The moral of the story is to do the job properly in the first place and you won't have to re-do it.

What's the saying on this? You've never got time to do the job properly but you can always find time to re-do it.

Ain't human nature a wonderful thing.

17 VINEYARD IMPLEMENTS TO MAKE LIFE EASIER

Slashers

We've been through two tractor mounted slashers. They take a beating and like any mechanical device, eventually they'll break.

The first one was a small offset designed to run right next to the vines. It was too small (only 4' wide) so it meant we did two runs to cut each row, but it came with the winery so we didn't complain too much.

The gearbox dropped a bearing and we figured this was the trigger we needed for an upgrade.

Next on the shopping list was a beautiful 6' bright red Waratah brand slasher which when I picked it up, hung over both sides of the trailer. We forklifted it off the trailer and hooked it up. And next came one of my more stupid novice type mistakes: I didn't check the oil in the gearbox before heading out into the vines.

Well, you can probably guess the outcome. I seized the gearbox solid. To their credit, the manufacturer replaced it under warranty and now I'm fanatical about oil levels in machinery. One of the staff destroyed a ride-on mower a few years back as he ignored our specific instructions: check the oil level *each time* before you start the mower.

Ouch...

Ouch for both my time repairing it and my wallet.

And we broke the gearbox on this slasher as well. It physically broke teeth in the gears. We used it to slash the vine rows, we used it to level blackberry infestations and clear the wilder parts of the property, so I guess it was only a matter of time before it cried uncle.

I welded the frame and replaced bolts holding the frame to the deck several times but, considering the work this slasher's done we sure got our moneys' worth.

The Side Throw Mower and Mulcher

This was one of the most useful bits of kit we ever bought. It's versatile, it works, it's flexible and it's bullet proof. Almost bullet proof that is.

It's a Chris Grow Engineering Vine Minder side throw mower/mulcher. These folks custom make each one to fit down your vine rows.

It's a tractor mount, PTO driven mower with two contra-rotating cutters. With the side plates removed it throws out both sides. So you drive down the vine row and it throws the cut grass out either side under the vine. It's one pass and it's done.

Now when you bolt in the side plates it becomes a mulcher. We used this to mulch the prunings as well as grass. The only downside of mulching the prunings is how LOUD it was. I'm wearing earplugs under the earmuffs and my ears were ringing for hours afterwards.

The only problem we had was with a popped oil seal on one of the gearboxes. It did the same seal on the same gearbox twice which was very annoying. The first time it seized a bearing but the second time we caught it in time. But the hours and hours of work to pull the gearbox out, clean it, take it away, have it fixed and then fit it all back was most annoying. And it only did this on the one gearbox, the other two survived years of use and abuse with no hassles.

It's the first (and thankfully only) design like this I've ever seen. The oil seal has no protection underneath, the blades are right there. Every other implement had some guard over the oil seals except this one. And this one was the one that was hardest to pull apart and fit back together.

It needed a lot of maintenance. As we're putting a lot of horsepower through it the clutch demanded regular adjustment and or replacement and the blades required sharpening to do their best in mulch mode.

And to replace the blades I'd have to grind the retaining bolts out as you can imagine the beating they took under the deck. Working underneath on this machine I'm covered in the crap, mud, clippings and everything else caught up under the deck. No matter how much you paid attention you'd set fire to the grass caught under there and you'd be patting it out with your hands while the ash was falling down your shirt. Putting the new ones in was a balancing act. I had my foot jammed against the rotor to stop it turning while I'm leaning all my weight on the wrench to tighten the bolts. When something slipped (as it often did for me) I've skinned my knuckles or crushed a finger yet again. It was dirty, hard and frustrating work to change them.

Power Harrows

Why would a winery use power harrows? More to the point what are power harrows? It's an implement that levels land and smashes up the soil to a fine consistency that's easy for plants to take to.

As much as we could do by machine, we did. This meant that we were spraying, picking, pruning, netting, under-vine sweeping and weed spraying all by machine. So the fewer bumps and holes in the ground the smoother the work was.

We regularly power-harrowed the vine rows and areas around the vines to smooth the land. It was easier on the operators and on the machinery. Instead of bouncing around and holding on for dear life, the operator could concentrate on their task.

It was slow going as the harrows do their best work inching along. This meant using the tractor creeper gears which give a ground speed between 400m and 1,500m per hour. The harrows are 2.15m wide so to cover a decent area takes time.

And they were heavy. They weighed several hundred kilograms and were an absolute bastard to hook up. If you didn't hit the 3PL (3 Point Linkage, which is the way you connect implements onto the tractors) dead centre onto them, then you'd be heaving and swearing with a crow bar to lever them onto the back. What was most annoying about this is that a 5 minute 'let's hook up the harrows and go' task turned into a 45 minute battle just to get to the point where you can start doing the job you set out to do.

The newer plantings were well laid out and one pass would level each vine row. I'm convinced the older vines we inherited were planted after a long boozy lunch. The vine rows varied from 2.75m out to 3.3m wide. You had to breathe in when working in the narrow rows and be super careful with any tractor implements. Don't pay attention for a split second and you'd drift off centre and hit a vine or post, meaning more damage that took me more time to fix. The wide rows meant that mowing, harrowing and the rest took two passes down the row, while the narrow rows meant the mulcher threw grass further out or the airblast sprayer drenched the vines. But, it's what we inherited and I wasn't going to pull out 25 year old vines just to fix this.

I drew flak from other winemakers about the harrows and my obsession with keeping the rows level. For us, it paid off as anything I could do to cut down equipment damage by staff was worth its weight in plutonium to me.

A lot of these tasks, such as spraying and mowing, are pure mindless 'sit there and watch the world go by' type jobs if you want them to be.

However, there was so much to see if you only kept your eyes open a tiny little bit. Sure, part of it comes back to having the 'owner's eyes' to see things. Other things came down to keeping your eyes open and having the interest and gratitude for the environment around you to observe nature at its finest.

The Kookaburras, a native Australian bird similar to a kingfisher, figured out very early in the piece that any time there was major tractor activity in the vineyard there was also a meal waiting. Slashing down the vine rows put me at eye level to the tops of the posts. The Kookaburras sat on the posts, calmly watching you drive past and then swept on whatever bug the slasher/mulcher threw out.

A pair of wedge tailed eagles nested somewhere nearby. These are monster eagles with a 6-8' (1.8m to 2.4m) wingspan and to watch them ride the thermals over the winery was a sight I never tired of. And, while the eagles were around, all other birds disappeared and hid in the safety of their trees. Birdsong stopped and an unnatural silence descended. Where 10 minutes earlier there were enough birds to make LAX look like an air traffic controllers Sunday picnic, now I had two beautiful creatures circling overhead, utterly alone and secure in their domain. When the drifted off to other hunting grounds the smaller birds eventually came out again and 15 minutes later the air was dense with birdsong once again.

We'd find birds' nests in the vines though I'm not sure how smart these birds were as the sprayer would send the nests flying. I assume that a few days uninterrupted is enough for most birds to build a nest and a few seconds sadly more than enough for us to destroy it.

Some 12 years of our time at the winery were drought years and the drier it was, the more the local wildlife saw the vineyard as a supermarket in the wilderness.

Unfortunately I can't find a photograph where the foxes came to take their share of the grapes. They chewed off the bottom of the low hanging bunches. There was a complete bunch with the few of the bottom most grapes picked clean off, looking like someone had grabbed a few grapes off the bottom and left the rest intact. It took a while to figure out what and who was doing this and in the end it's simply another part of nature doing what it needs to survive.

Perhaps the most bizarre thing we saw, or rather felt, in the vines was a snake. Peter K was summer pruning in the shiraz and felt what he described as a sharp stick hitting him on his upper thigh. He came down to the sheds and the tell-tale two fang marks had started to welt up. We made a frantic dash to the local doctor who confirmed it was a snake bite and immediately directed us to the local hospital. Even with breaking the speed limit as much as the car could, it was close to an hour before Peter K was in the emergency room. They took blood samples, swabs, more samples and dragged in every intern in the place for a look to witness a real live snake bite. A few hours passed with no ill effect other than a massive adrenalin overdose and Peter K was released.

We drove back to the winery at a much more sedate rate, ignored the pruning and got stuck into the wines to celebrate another brush with death.

It seems amazing now that we could be an hour from help. A new 24/7 ambulance station opened a mere 10km from the winery in 2011 but 17 years ago we were in the wild, wild west.

And another drought related truly bizarre thing was the peeled lemons. The front winery house had a beautiful old Meyer lemon tree giving wonderful fruit over several months of the year. Along with the heritage apples you could feast off for months, the place was a slow food delight. During some of the driest months we lived through I noticed a few lemons hanging on the tree that were missing their skin. They were still attached to the tree, perfectly healthy but also perfectly peeled and perfectly hanging there with only the flesh attached to the stalk, no skin. After asking the older neighbours I found it was possums looking for moisture that'd often eat the skins off citrus trees. I was ready to blame the kids or go get the shotgun, but here was Mother Nature having yet another joke at my expense.

Anyway, enough about the power harrows…

Sprayer

Step one is to share our philosophy on chemicals in the vineyard. We kept the vineyard as close to organic as geographically possible. By geographically possible I mean as close as we could get in cold climate region with other vineyards close by. We didn't go down the organic path as, in our location we would have harvested one crop out of ten.

As well as the local vineyards, about 20km upwind was another large wine region. If one vineyard there missed one spray we got every mould and mildew back within the hour. So we took the middle route using a Bordeaux mix to coat the grape with a protective copper and sulphur layer and avoid the systemic fungicides. There were times the weather and Mother Nature had us using fungicides, but thankfully they were few. It did mean we sprayed more often than if we had been using systemic fungicides but for us it was worth it. Our cold climate meant we were spraying more often than the warmer wine regions, but that was our choice and you work with what you've got. We made clean and low preservative wines and people loved them and kept coming back for them.

We used no broad range pesticides ever.

None, not one.

Full stop and amen.

And we were lucky to have very few out of control insect pests and it's worth having a look at each one and the reasons why.

Snail control comes down to basic vineyard hygiene during spring. We used an under vine weed spray after harvest and by spring time the grass was dying. With the grass dying, there was nowhere for the snails to breed and live so hence no snails. In the few early years when we missed the weed sprays we'd go through the vines and pick the snails from the crown and crush them on the ground. It was a lot of work, it took a long time, but it was better than dumping chemicals onto the vineyard.

Blister mites were the next easiest thing to 'fix'. Blister mites are tiny mites that cause water drop size blisters or bubbles on the vine leaf. Each blister reduces the efficiency of each leaf so the vine has to work harder to harvest the sunlight. The leaf's still there but it looks like it's covered in blisters and isn't doing its work. The utter irony here was that the less we did, the fewer blister mites we had. It was sound natural balance practice or the fancy name conjured up by folks wanting to cash in on this 'trend' is IPM, Integrated Pest Management. The conventional wisdom says to spray lime sulphur prior to budburst and, while this works for the mites, it also destroys every other bug in the vineyard. And it reeks. The lime sulphur smells disgusting and it coats everything with a fine white layer of muck. The more spiders, ladybirds and other little critters we had in the vineyard, the less blister mite damage we got.

That's not some idiot wanker urban greenie spewing mindless rhetoric. That's plain observed and recorded fact.

This is a really key point so I'll say it again. The more natural predators we had in the vineyards, which were there because we didn't spray any broad range pesticides, the less harmful insect mass infestations we had. We had a sound natural balance.

The AWRI (Australian Wine Research Institute) people developed 'good' predatory mites to provide a biological control but frankly, after we stopped spraying the conventional fix we never had enough of a problem to use them. As clean and as green as we could be worked best for us.

The last bug on the list in our area was the light brown apple moth, LBAM for short. The moth stage caused no problems but the caterpillar stage did. Well I can't really say less than 1% chewed leaf is grief, but it didn't look good and would've impacted the vine efficiency. Luckily once again a biological control came to the rescue. A few grams of this control in each spray would kill just the LBAM caterpillars and nothing else. It was a great solution.

We started with a Hardi brand crop sprayer. That was a conventional tractor mounted 400L sprayer, PTO driven to pump spray out both sides of the vertical booms. Depending on the length of canes on the vines I'd use anywhere from 4 to all 10 jets. Obviously the more jets I used, the more often I was filling the tank so the longer each spray took. All I needed was one hiccup and I'd miss the still mornings and the wind would come up. So I'd have to go back out the next morning and finish the spray.

It worked, it did what we asked from it and I did a lot of maintenance to keep it going and working. I had to spend an hour prior to each spray dismantling the nozzles and cleaning the jets as even the smallest bit of dirt in there meant a jet would clog and then the application rate was way out. When I thought I'd put down the right amount and found I had half a tank left, I'd start swearing and head out again to go over what I'd just 'finished'.

Next on the list was an airblast sprayer. This was the latest and greatest technology touted at the field days so it was time to update.

An airblast sprayer is another tractor mounted sprayer with a huge fan pushing air out at some 200kph. Or at least the brochure says 200kph and that felt about right. It radically changed the way we sprayed and the time it took and the amount of spray we put out. I could spray faster and sleep easier as I knew, I absolutely knew each part of the vine was covered. Especially at bunch closure time, I knew I had my anti botrytis sprays in and ready to go. The super fine droplets that were thrown out coated everything in the blast stream with a consistent layer of 'muck': leaves, bunches, wires and posts all got an equal non-discriminatory dose.

The great thing about the airblast sprayer was the minute droplets driven by 200kph fans. The only real hassle with the airblast sprayer was the 200kph wind. It meant that any under-vine mulch was blown away as soon as I came near it. Even grass clippings would be flying away.

I always wore disposable overalls and full face mask while spraying. Most of the sprays were harmless, but I'd rather be paranoid than sick. During summer it got pretty hot and sticky and sweaty as I only had an open/ROPS tractor, not one with a full air conditioned detox cabin.

Mixing the chemicals and filling the tank took time. All the chemicals we used could be tank mixed, but not overnight. That meant I would start the tank filling with the tractor running to agitate the mix. As the level in the tank went up I'd add in each component and let them mix in. It took about 40 minutes to fill each tank and then about an hour to empty it.

The final word on vine sprays? We had a windy site. When we were in the spray 'window', I would be up early every morning and when it was still and rain free for 8+ hours I would go and keep going. The times when each day got wetter and windier and I just couldn't get out spraying were maddening and stressful and had you cursing at anything that moved. Fortunately they were few and far between.

It's hard to describe the utter helplessness and soul wrenching frustration when you know you have mildews thriving on the leaves and you have all the resources ready to fix it but Mother Nature just kept on raining and blowing and keeping you away.

Some vintages we lost part of the crop due to bad weather and mildews. That's a risk we knew we had and we accepted it as part of growing wine grapes in a cold climate to produce clean, low preservative wines.

Undervine Sweeper

Another tool in the toolbox of vineyard hygiene was a huge spinning broom called an undervine sweeper. When the sweeper worked well, it worked like a charm and ticked along giving me great results. When it didn't work it had me throwing a tantrum like a 2 year-old at bedtime.

The sweeper hooked onto the 3PL and needed one full flow hydraulic remote. Think of a big street sweeper spinning broom hanging off the back of the tractor whose purpose was to sweep the prunings out from under the vines into the alley way so they'd get mulched.

The setup was fiddly and when we got it right it worked a treat. I'd merrily idle along in 1st gear, high range on the tractor with the sweeper spinning behind me.

But when I wasn't watching or lost concentration I'd glance back to find rolls of irrigation pipe wrapped around the broom. Then it's time to untangle it, finish the job I was doing and come back to repair the irrigation. One of the staff destroyed a section of irrigation and, not wanting to tell me, replaced the pipe while I was away. But he didn't replace the drippers so come summer I'm wondering where the water is? Just another task to do…

The brushes were flexible enough to get the canes out but not rough enough to rip out weeds or strip off suckers. And they lasted about two seasons before wearing out.

And the reason we used it?

It comes back to vineyard hygiene. The first few years we dragged out the prunings and burnt them each season. Conventional wisdom and built up diseases (botrytis over-winters on the canes) in the vines dictated we do this. After the first few years the vineyard was disease free and we started mulching the prunings back in rather than destroying the nutrients. The vineyard got healthier and healthier and vines got better and better.

When I'd missed a weed spray and I had weeds under the vines the sweeper missed some of the prunings. It was no huge problem, although the vineyard looked utterly fantastic when it was clean and green and freshly mowed.

Weed Sprayer

We got the weed sprays right after 5 different versions of the spray kit.

Number one was a hand spray run by a basic PTO driven roller pump fed from a 200 litre (44 gallon) drum riding on the carryall behind the tractor. It came with the place, it worked most of the time but it was a pain in the arse the rest of the time. Needless to say it didn't last long.

The next version was a low volume dome shielded sprayer bolted to the quad bike fed by an electric pump and a 50 litre (10 gallon) tank. It worked a treat, it used very little chemical and you could spray with a typhoon blowing around you. But it was soooooo slooooooow I'd be falling asleep on the bike and my hand was cramping holding the throttle steady.

The next iteration replaced the low volume part with a handheld wand using the same tank and pump. This was much, much faster and chemical use was the same. The only downside was the frequent refills since we were going so much faster.

After this we outsourced the vineyard management to a contractor for a few years. This was a total disaster and ended up costing us a lot of money, lost grape, lower quality grape and weeds growing up past the fruit wire. It seemed like a cost-effective good idea at the time but, with that most wonderful of human traits, hindsight, we should have gotten rid of this dickhead contractor a lot sooner than we did. He sprayed with a tractor mounted sprayer, when he turned up that is, killing a lot of grass before and after the vine row and the vineyard looked like crap while he was there. Enough said…

The final version came as a 200 litre trailer-mounted, electric-driven spray tank towed by a quad bike. It was quick, I'd be out spraying for a few hours between refills and I wish we'd done this a long time ago.

There were many things where we'd stand back and say 'why didn't we do this 10 years ago'?

This was one of them.

Ride on Mowers

Here's another case of fifth time lucky. Mower version number 5 was quick, fast, efficient and left a great looking lawn.

Originally we started with some lawn around the house and a little bit of non-jungle in front of the winery. Rustic is the nicest way I can describe the grounds we inherited. I'm using 'rustic' here the same way a real estate agent uses 'renovator's delight' to describe a home that should've been bulldozed many years ago.

A push mower for the lawns and the tractors out in the vines worked for a while.

Soon enough the gardens started spreading so we ended up with more lawns.

Our first ride-on mower was a broken down, second hand bargain. Money was tight for us and we thought a fixer-upper was the way to go. Well, we got it working, we got it cutting, but parts kept falling off faster than we could bolt them back on so we traded this on a new 36" cut Masport.

The Masport was designed for civilised urban lawns and not the wilds of the winery. And to be fair to the poor little beastie it gave a good fight right to the bitter end. We beat the hell out of it while at the same time nurturing it till we traded it for a nice, shiny new bright red 38" cut Toro.

The Toro felt magnificent. The hydrostatic transmission meant no more shifting gears, the wider cut turned grass turn to lawn in half the time and the extra power felt like we could take on any jungle. Somewhere in the world there's a Toro engineer who felt their underwear tighten up several times a week. They don't know why and they never will. Well, it was me tugging on their jocks. The sheer amount of work we did with this little machine would've made any engineer weep into their breakfast cereal if they knew what we'd done to their creation. When there was more weld metal in the deck than original metal it was time for another upgrade.

We went one more size up with a 42" from Husqvarna this time. And it felt like jumping from a toy to a tractor. But unfortunately the rough ground, the sticks, the stones and all other crap we run over in the country soon had me welding the deck again. The Husky gave a marvellous cut and finish but these ride-ons are designed for suburban lawns and not the acres and acres of paddock and lawn we were cutting. When we sold this, the top half was immaculate but the deck looked like it had been used for target practice by the Taliban.

The final one was the biggest and best and fastest and toughest. We bought a 61" cut zero turn Ferris with almost as much horsepower as the tractors. The deck was solid metal rather than pressed sheet steel, it had suspension, a rollbar and two fuel tanks. And it was quick. A block of vines that took us 45 minutes to cut with the Husky or the tractors took 11 (eleven) minutes with the new Ferris.

Another part of the gardens with a lot of large trees that took me 3-4 hours with the tractor was done in 1 hour. The speed and capacity and manoeuvrability were like jumping off a bicycle onto a motorbike.

It was one of those things that we should have done many years ago but didn't have the money. And once again I wondered how we'd survived without it and suddenly the investment of money vs time spent on the old mowers made the money seem irrelevant.

18 OVERSEAS VINEYARDS

Germany

I got the chance to see the vineyards around Rudesheim and realised how lucky we were as winemakers in Australia.

In Australia we design our vineyards around the turning circle of the largest tractor we have. We set vine rows 3m apart to fit a full size tractor and whatever implements we have. The headlands are obstacle free for at least 10m so we can turn any tractor. But here was a country where vineyard land is so scarce and costly that every square centimetre is planted.

The spacing between vine rows floored me.

How do you spray?

How do you net?

How do you harvest?

Mostly by hand is the answer. This seemed insane to me and that's about the time I first truly appreciated how good we have it in Australia. We don't have 400 years of tradition and archaic laws restricting what can be planted in what regions and how much we are permitted to harvest per acre. What a load of crap.

It's this freedom to experiment that's produced Australian world beating wines. Grange is the best known example of stunning results when you go against tradition. And what about sparkling shiraz? If you've never tasted this, then please do your tastebuds a favour and go hunt down a bottle now. It's this free-to-try-new-technologies-and-methods environment that's put Australia on the world wine map. Otherwise, how could a country producing less than 2% of world wine come up with so many stunning wines?

Germany is the physical home to riesling, have a look at this history article I put together many years ago;

The history of the riesling vine can be traced back to Germany and the year 1435. The first documented evidence comes from the cellar log of Count Katzenelnbogen at Ruesselsheim on 13th March 1435. Klaus Kleinfish sold the Count six riesling vines for the sum of 22 solidi. There are other supposed 'first plantings' but without the documented evidence: Wachau in Austria in 1232, Alsace in 1348 and Westhofen in Rheinhessen in 1402. An undocumented tale of riesling from the 14th century has the Cistercian Monks at Eberbach disappointed in their light Rheingau reds compared to the French reds. Their instruction to their growers to remove all plantings other than the white vines ensured the spread of the riesling vine. In 1464 the St Jacob Hospice in Trier purchased 1,200 'Ruesseling' vines. 1490 sees another reference to 'Ruessling hinder Kirssgarten' (riesling behind the cherry orchard) and a 'Risslingwingart' at Pfeddersheim in 1511 shows that riesling was starting to spread.

The name riesling seems a bit harder to clarify. 'Russ' means dark wood and this along with the grooved bark gives the resultant root word 'rissig'. Another likely reference relates to riesling's poor flowering in cold weather which is described by the German words 'verrieseln' or 'durchrieseln'.

Hieronymus Bock refers to riesling in 1552 and also in a later version of his book on herbs in 1577 he mentions riesling growing in 'the Mosel, the Rhein and the environs or Worms'. In 1716 the Prince-Abbey of Fulda purchased the rundown Benedictine Abbey in Johannisberg in the Rheingau. 294,000 riesling vines from Ruedesheim, Eberbach, and Floersheim were planted during 1720 to 1721 to replace the neglected plantings. Clemens Wenzeslaus, Elector of Trier, on 8th May 1787 proclaimed at all inferior vines be dug up and replanted with noble (riesling) varieties. By the end of the 19th century riesling was the dominant variety in the Rheingau and was significant in the rest of Germany.

The early 20th century saw riesling declining in Germany with only 57% of the Rheingau planted to riesling in 1930. This trend was reversed during the rest of the century and now riesling is treated as a national treasure. The push is now to think of riesling in Germany as you do Pinot Noir and chardonnay in Burgundy or cabernet sauvignon in Bordeaux.

The first reference to riesling in Australia is in 1820. William Macarthur planted 20 acres of vineyards at Camden Park near Penrith in NSW. The commercial plantings included: Pineau Gris, Frontignac, Gouais, Verdelho, cabernet sauvignon, riesling, Grenache and Mataro. October 1837 sees Johann Stein and 5 other 'vinedressers' arrive in Australia from Germany under a 5-year contract with William Macarthur and successfully introduce Rhine riesling into Australia.

Penfolds Wines purchases 'Minchinbury' in 1912 and expands the vineyards to over 400 acres of old and new varieties including: Verdelho, riesling, Cabernet riesling, Pinot Noir, Hermitage, Traminer and Pinot Blanc. Then we come to the 1970's where the combination of the new invention called the wine cask and sweet fruity styles such as Gewürztraminer, Gewürztraminer riesling, and Rhine riesling ensured the riesling boom in Australia. Incidentally, Angoves first introduced the wine cask in 1965.

The legend of sweet riesling is generally accredited to Schloss Johannisberg in the Rheingau who 'accidentally' created their first 'Spatlese' or late harvest in 1775. The legend goes that the messenger bringing the official order to start picking was robbed on the way. By the time he arrived the grapes had rotted, been infected with Botrytis and were given to the peasants. The peasants brewed their own wonderful wines and the rest is history.

It's the riesling grapes ability to develop high sugar levels while maintaining acidity that produces white wines that age very well. riesling is produced from dry to very sweet. The sweet, botrytis affected wines are rated in ascending order of sweetness as: Auslese, Beerenauslese and Trockenbeerenauslese.

riesling means different things to different people. In Australia the word riesling has traditionally referred to any sweet wine variety. Stricter labelling laws now ensure that when you see riesling on the label you do get riesling. riesling has suffered the unfortunate association with sweet, white cask wine. Only the last ten years or so has seen riesling coming back into fashion as a crisp, clean white winedrink. The lime and citrus flavours in the cooler climate rieslings make a wonderful summer drink.

A true riesling in California is referred to as a Johannisberg riesling. Gray riesling and Emerald rieslings are different varieties and Sylvaner is commonly called Sylvaner riesling, Franken riesling, Monterey riesling and even Sonoma riesling. Parts of Europe have a Welschriesling or Italian riesling but this is a different variety. South Africans have Cape riesling, Clare riesling, Paarl riesling and South African riesling which are all really Cruchen Blanc. Weisser riesling is what you have to look for to find a true riesling. Even in rieslings homeland Germany, Schwarzriesling is in reality the variety Müllerrebe (Meunier) and the variety Rulander is called Grauer riesling.

And to confuse matters even more, there are several riesling hybrids of which the most famous is a cross between riesling and Sylvaner called Müller-Thurgau. Other names that riesling answers to in Germany include: Johannisberger, Klingelberger, riesling Renano, and White riesling.

And it's not just the vines that have different names. The wine itself has many names in different countries including: Italy (riesling Italico); Austria (Welschriesling); Hungary (OlaszRizling); Rumania (riesling de Italic); Bulgaria (ItalianskyRizling); Yugoslavia (Laski Rizling); Czechoslovakia (RizlingVlassky) and Russia (RislingItalianski)

I was dumbfounded to find so many riesling bunches riddled with Botrytis. Surely the home of riesling can do better?

Anyway, seeing the home of riesling was a full on religious experience for me. So much history and such magnificent vineyards. It makes you want to go make some serious wines…

Latvia

My parents came to Australia from Latvia after WWII and I got a chance to visit Latvia after the Iron Curtain came down.

Naturally I hit every wine shop and wine bar I could find. And yes there were plenty of great Australian wines lining the shelves but the real surprise was finding a vineyard in a place that sees minus 20C temperatures and metres of winter snow.

The vineyard at Sabile, or the Wine Hill of Sabile as it's called, is recognised by the Guinness World Record people as the most northern vineyard in the world.

Here was a vineyard where every operation is done by hand in total contrast to us where we do everything by machine. The Sabile vineyard's about 1 acre in size and by contrast our front lawn is larger than that.

It was a culture shock to say the least and drove home again how powerful the link with wine is in any culture.

This is the history;

The Wine Hill of Sabile has been formed twice (for the first time in the German period 14th-16thcenturies) but after that it has been started completely all over again in the period of the first Latvian free state.

In the time of the Duke Jacob the vine crop in Sabile is supplemented with new sorts and the vine cultivation is developing. From the middle of 17th century the formation of Sabile's Wine Hill is celebrated.

The strong and sourish wine of Sabile's Wine Hill has been very popular in the courts of Kurzeme Duchy and also in other countries of Europe where it has been exported.

Rebirth of Sabile's Wine Hill started in 1936. It is mentioned in different sources that the initiative has come from the then president of Latvia Karlis Ulmanis. The proof that Wine Hill has been developed and yielded in the time of the first Latvian free state, was the grape exhibition in Jelgava, 1939, which was organized by Latvian Agriculture Company. There was also a small stand of the first harvest of Sabile's Wine Hill.

But then the Second World War began and further development of Sabile's Wine Hill was interrupted. After the war the Gardening and experimental Station of Pure continued to arrange the vineyard. But then the managers of it changed again as a consequence the quality of work decreased. After all the Wine Hill was not taken care of at all.

In 1989 a group of enthusiastic students started a renovation of Sabile's Wine Hill.

Today the height of the Wine Hill is 33.7m (about 115feet above sea level). The total area of the vineyard is 1.5ha.

The Wine Hill of Sabile was honoured by the visit of ex-president of Latvia Guntis Ulmanis who planted an apple tree at the foot of the hill.

The plantations in the vineyard are regularly supplemented. There are about 650 vines of 15 different sorts. The well-known Latvian selectionist Pauls Sukatnieks has developed most of them. Soft 'Zilga' forms the majority of vines.

Not only vines can be found in the Wine Hill, there are also some things a little more exotic – peach, apricots, and walnut-trees.

19 GETTING READY FOR VINTAGE

Processing - Wine Barrel History

Before we slide into the processing, let's have a look at where the wine barrel came from and why it's the size it is.

The ancient Greeks and Italians seemed happy to ship their wines in rather fragile amphorae. Herodotus refers to palm-wood casks used in shipping Armenian wine to Babylon in Mesopotamia, but it is really during the iron age and the northern Europeans, the Celts in particular, who developed the wooden barrel for transporting goods.

The wine barrel was traditionally used for storage and transportation of goods. Now it's almost exclusively used in the production of fine wines and spirits. The barrel is traditionally referred to as a keg when empty and cask when full. I'll use barrels to be consistent.

The capacity of a barrel comes from both practical experience and historical 'capacity'. A generally agreed assumption relates the volume of the barrel to the amount of grapes harvested from a set piece of land.

A 'sadon' was an area of around 830 m2 having some 900 vines, as French vines are planted much more densely than Australian ones. A worker would be allotted a 'wadge' when he had cut back and tied the area, thus a 'sadon' wage. The harvest would generally yield around 450 litres per 'sadon'. Two barrels per 'sadon', approx 225 litres per barrel.

Another popular barrel size is the Borgogne (Burgundy) barrel at 228 litres. It's safe to say that barrels from different regions were somewhere between 200 and 230 litres depending on the amount harvested and what wine could be made from the harvest.

The 225 litre Bordeaux barrel is the most widely used size today and its common name is the barrique. Its dimensions are 940 to 945 mm in length, 550 to 555 mm in diameter in head and 690 to 695 mm in diameter in what is named the dump or bilge. The chateau Bordeaux has staves around 22 mm thick while the more robust transport Bordeaux uses 27 mm staves.

The chateau Bordeaux is a very elegant barrel, often having wicker and chestnut bracing across the head. The Borgogne (at one time found only in Burgundy) is 228 litres in capacity and slightly shorter and wider than the Bordeaux while still having the robust 27 mm staves. A Hogshead is around 300 litres while a Puncheon is around 400 litres in capacity.

Each cooper may have their own variations in sizes, but the traditional Bordeaux and Borgogne barrels will be found anywhere.

A typical barrel is a 225 litre barrique made from French oak.

The MEDIUM stencilled on the head of the barrel refers to the toasting. Traditionally heat was applied only to bend the staves and form the barrel until someone noticed the different levels of heating and charring inside the barrel produced different wine flavours. It's now generally accepted to use three levels of toasting: light, medium and medium plus. The winemaker specifies the level of toasting required when ordering a new barrel as well as the type of oak.

A Glossary of Wine Barrel Terms

This glossary sums up the most common terms associated with wine barrels.

Air Dry – Oak is dried out in the open for a few years for barrel production rather than kiln dried as used for construction timber.

Barre - This refers to the wooden bar crossing both heads of Bordeaux Chateau style barrels. These barres are ornamental in function rather than structural.

Barrel - Any wooden vessel having bent sides and flat ends. Synonymous with cask, barrique (Bordeaux) and fut (Burgundy).

Bung - A wooden plug that goes into the bunghole. Now more common for this to be silicon rather than wood

Bilge - The centre of the barrel where it has its largest diameter.

Cask – Used interchangeably with barrel.

Chamfer - The sloping ends of the staves.

Charring – The blackening on the inside of the barrel as it is heated over an open fire after it's bent to shape. A certain degree of toasting occurs as a normal result of the manufacturing process as the staves are bent.

Chime - The end of the stave at the head of the barrel. The part of the stave where the groove and chamfer are cut.

Cooper - A skilled craftsperson who has learned the trade of barrel making through an apprenticeship or formal cooperage program.

Cooperage - The production facility where the barrels are made (the French term is Tonnellerie).

Croze - The groove at the end of the stave or barrel cut to accommodate the head boards

Dowels - Small round wooden or metal pins or pegs used to join heading pieces together.

Esquive - Smaller bung hole on the barrel head used for racking wine, typically located either at the 6 o'clock or 8 o'clock position, but I've never seen one in Australia.

Flagging – Ornamental dried rush, hickory or river reed used in the fabrication of barrel heads.

Heads - The flat ends of a barrel or vat. The pieces of wood forming the heads are called head pieces or head staves.

Hoops - The strips of metal or chestnut wood used to hold the barrel together. Galvanized steel is the most common material used with the ends of each strip riveted together.

Hoop Driver - The tool used, together with a hammer, to force down the hoops to make the barrel tight.Now done by machine.

Shaving – The removal of 1 – 3mm of the inside of the barrel to expose a fresh wood surface.

Spiles - Small wooden conical- shaped pegs used to seal holes and stop leaks in barrels.

Staves - The pieces of wood used for the sides of a barrel (in which case they are bent) or a tank. The term is used for the rough-cut material before it is processed, as well as the finished product. The French term is douelle.

Toasting - See "Charring"

Tank - Any large wooden vessel having straight sides. It is also called a vat.

Barrels and Stakvats

A wonderful Australian invention called a Stakvat hit the wine scene some years ago. It's a 900 litre stainless steel cube with oak sides.

Wine and vineyards in Australia don't have hundreds of years of tradition and bizarre laws telling us what we can and can't do. In parts of Europe you're limited as to how much you can crop per acre of vines and what varieties you can plant. In Australia, as long as you're safe and clean, the sky's pretty much the limit on what you can do and experiment with.

The boom in Australian wines over the last 40 years was fuelled by these new wines. Wines that clobbered the old world 'masters' with magnificent fruit and clean flavours that left much of Europe drowning in their own wine lake. Just look at Grange and Hill of Grace as good examples of what you get from Australia.

Anyway, Stakvats were a revelation for us.

Our goal was to produce clean wines. By that I mean as low as possible in preservatives, sulphur and other additives. Not organic as that brought a whole new swag of problems with it. But clean, low preservative wines that people loved to drink.

The advantages Stakvats had for us included:

Much cleaner - We could swing open an entire side and steam clean every square inch. To clean a barrel you must get inside through a 2" hole. How is that helping keep things clean? Keeping barrels clean was a nightmare for us and we were glad to get rid of them. Stakvats were a life, time and sanity saver.

Better oak quality per dollar - Oak becomes a wine barrel through the black art of cooperage. Each stave is shaped, bent and individually matched to the barrel. So obviously the craftsman's touch is a huge part of the cost. Stakvats use straight oak battens so there's no expensive, rare and skilled craftsman producing them. And this meant we could use newer, higher quality oak as it was cheaper to replace.

No manual handling issues - An empty, wet barrel weighs around 40kg. Add in over 220 litres of wine and we're looking at a quarter of a ton. Barrels were a nightmare to move around. By comparison we'd forklift a Stakvat and put it wherever we wanted. Empty, full, two high or whatever. They were a breeze to move with the forklift.

Storage space - We found once you'd put a barrel onto the racks and filled it there was no way you'd move it till it was empty. Space in the winery and coolrooms was always stretched but we'd easily pick up and shuffle around the Stakvats and this made life much easier.

Same wine to oak surface area ratio - The Stakvats had the same wine to oak surface area ratio. That meant we had no learning curve to go from barrels to Stakvats when it came to oak maturation which meant an easy swap over.

New sides for the Stakvats arrived in a flat pack. This is all they were; flat packs of straight oak pieces and not intricate masterpieces. It was surprising how cheap top quality oak was before it got to the cooper.

One question we always got was about the capacity. If it's 900 litres then how do you know you'll always have 900 litres of wine to fill them? It's the same argument you get about barrels, tanks, bins, whatever. And the answer we found was that it just didn't matter. No matter how carefully we'd plan, measure or do, we'd always have the wrong amount. There was just too much or a tad too little. So you work around it and get on with what you're doing. Nothing's ever going to be perfect and as we found it would rarely be even close to perfect.

If it meant keeping wine back in stainless steel a little longer, then that's what we did. If it meant that we'd blend a few hundred litres of un-oaked wine in with several thousand litres of oaked wine, well that's what we did.

I learnt a lot about patience and a lot about working with less than ideal situations and tools and outcomes, but...

We won medals for wine oaked in barrels and we won medals for wines oaked in Stakvats. So from our experience and the evidence we stuck to the Stakvats.

And, variable capacity stainless steel tanks were definitely God's gift to winemakers.

Cleaning

We spent at least the same amount of time (and usually more) cleaning than we would actually 'doing' what it was that we'd cleaned for.

That includes cleaning before you're 'doing' as the kit has to be clean. After all you're working with a foodstuff. It's not like you're making furniture, you're making something that you'll be drinking, something that you'll be putting into your body. So you clean before you start and you clean it properly.

Then you do whatever it is you're doing. Be it filtering, blending, pressing, crushing, settling, transferring, bottling or whatever.

And then we'd repeat the cleaning process again once we'd finished.

We set our direction of producing clean, low preservative wines which meant using chemical cleaners wasn't on the menu but the equipment still had to be clean.

So, we bought a large, expensive diesel heated steam cleaner and it got a lot of use. It was brilliant to work with and it got as much use cleaning down the tractors and sprayers as it did in the winery. The steam setting disinfected everything before we started. The hot water setting gave us much more water flow which was great for cleaning the sprayers, oily tractors and sticky harvesters. There wasn't much that resisted 99C temperature and 3,000psi pressure hot water. The cold water setting didn't get much use as the other two were so easy to work with.

We spent so very much time cleaning that the concrete in front of the winery wore away.

The cleaning got really hard in the middle of winter. The wind was blowing, it was drizzling, your fingers were numb from the wet and cold and you're thinking to yourself: "are we having fun yet?" Yeah, I know you're asking why we didn't wear gloves etc, but they just got in the way for most things.

Then on the hot summer days you welcomed the fine spray blowing back on you to give a tiny little respite from the heat.

It was one of the most used and most useful bits of kit we had on the property.

Crusher De-stemmer

The very first crusher we had was Dads' hand driven antique dating from a time when dinosaurs still roamed the earth. It worked fine while we were backyard winemakers but was never cut out for the commercial world.

The first motorised version came with the winery and while it worked, I can't say it was effective or elegant or much of anything else. It now sits in the garden filled with plants and that's by far the most appropriate place for it.

The crusher de-stemmer was another great example of 'you get what you pay for'. The simple little ones we used early on clogged up and stuffed up when you fed through too much grape at a time. And that 'too much' amount was a very small amount.

They were temperamental with full bunches. The earlier ones just wouldn't feed a whole bunch. So we had to poke and prod it with a stick or dump a whole lot more grapes on top and hope this forced it through.

So you can better understand the frustrations with kit that didn't work let me paint the picture on the entire process. We used the crusher de-stemmer only during harvest. A typical day started by manually hauling off the nets which in itself was enough to stuff you for the day. Even with the later motorised net winders and feeders, it's a very, very physically hard task.

Now we had the nets off and we'd let the pickers in. They'd work down the rows and leave the fruit in foam boxes tucked under the vines. Well most of the time they'd leave them under the vines, sometimes they'd leave the boxes sticking out just far enough that you'd have to get off the quad bike, move the box aside, get back on, drive another 15 feet, get off, load the boxes and repeat this up and down the rows. The average box weighs 3-5kg and, while this isn't much weight, after you'd picked up hundreds of them, believe me you're feeling it.

Then we finally get to the winery, unload the boxes and start feeding them through the crusher de-stemmer. Sometimes we'd unload them onto pallets and store them in the cool room overnight. Other times we'd process them as they came in.

At this stage it's towards the end of the day. I'm hot, sweaty, tired and cranky at whatever else went wrong. There are people everywhere as invariably a tourist coach pulled in unloading another 48 tourists with cameras and questions. Now I'm battling with a piece of machinery holding up the entire process because I can't feed my grape through. Unless you've been there you won't and can't understand the frustration at this stage.

And you know what? I wouldn't trade a single hour of the frustrations and aches and pains for anything. They're memories and experiences not many people get and those memories and experiences flood back to me every time I swirl a glass of wine. The sights, the smells, the aches, the frustrations, they disappear with that magic first sip of your wine.

Anyway...

The next size up crusher de-stemmer worked sort of ok after we built a feeder chute around it. It would still jam up at random times for random reasons but it put us that one magic step closer to the stress free vintage.

I can't recall the exact number but crusher de-stemmer approximately number 5 finally worked without a hitch. It cost a lot to buy, it was huge, it ran off 3-phase power (via a generator) and boy did it work well. Finally we had the luxury of equipment that worked with us and not against us. We were the bottleneck in the process not the equipment and that was simply a lovely place to be.

And, for some pure trivia...

The reason for people 'stomping' on grapes rather than feeding them through some machinery has a sound practical basis. Where a machine may break open the seeds, the pressure generated by a bare human foot is enough to break open the grape but not enough to break open the seed. The seeds give a very tart bitter taste if they're broken. So, one of the key settings on the crusher de-stemmer was to set the rollers far enough apart to break open the grape but not crush the seed.

Adding the Yeast

Walking into the winery during vintage and having the yeasty ferment smell hit you in the face like a cricket bat was one of life's best moments. We were sore and bruised and usually limping from some knock or strain during harvest, but… no matter how tough the vintage, how hard it's been and how many things have gone pear shaped, that smell made it all worthwhile.

Before we go on here's a short history and science lesson on yeasts.

The difference between a bottle of grape juice and a bottle of wine is the alcohol, but where does the alcohol come from?

Alcohol results from the fermentation process where a micro- organism (yeast) converts sugar into alcohol and carbon dioxide gas. Yeast is a living organism critical to winemaking. Without yeast, there would be no beer, wine or spirits, bread, yoghurt or cheese.

"God is Good" was how yeast was referred to prior to 1859 when Louis Pasteur discovered that a single cell organism was responsible for the conversion of sugars into alcohol and carbon dioxide.

The Egyptians were the earliest recorded users of yeasts. They brewed wine and they baked bread.

Yeasts are around 6-8 microns in size. It takes about 20 billion of them to make up 1 gram of yeast and the chemical reaction that happens is $C_6H_{12}O_6 + yeast = 2C_2H_5OH + 2CO_2$.

Yeast is grown commercially by starting with a known 'strain' of yeast, feeding it with molasses or other sugars so it multiplies and then harvesting it.

Freeze dried yeast is the most popular form of yeast for wine making. It's kept in the fridge till required. The yeast is 're-hydrated' by adding it to water at 40°C and letting it stand for 20-30 minutes. Then it's tipped into the must to start the ferment.

There are hundreds of different yeasts for making wine. Yeasts occur naturally on the skin of grapes but we kill those off before fermentation. These wild yeasts would give unpredictable results and who knows what flavour you'd end up with. The winemaker decides what results he wants before the fermentation is started.

An example of one winemaking yeast and the information available to the winemaker is shown below. Lalvin is the manufacturer and ICV D-47 is the name of this yeast.

LALVIN (Dry) Wine Yeast Specifications ICV D-47
Origin

This strain was isolated from grapes grown in the Côtes-du-Rhône region of France by Dr. Dominique Delteil, head of the Microbiology Department, Institutcoopératif du vin (ICV), in Montpellier. ICV D-47 strain was selected from 450 isolates collected between 1986 and 1990.

OENOLOGICAL PROPERTIES AND APPLICATIONS

The ICV D-47 is a low-foaming quick fermenter that settles well, forming a compact lees at the end of fermentation. This strain tolerates fermentation temperatures ranging from 10° to 30°C (50° to 86°F) and enhances mouthfeel due to complex carbohydrates. Malolactic fermentation proceeds well in wine made with ICV D-47.

This strain is recommended for making wines from white varieties such as chardonnay and Rosé. It is also an excellent choice for producing mead, however be sure to supplement with yeast nutrients, especially usable nitrogen.

And the things that you have to put on an Australian alcohol product label include:

Under Australian law a 'product' must include a statement of the percentage by volume of ethanol therein at 20°C, expressed to the nearest first decimal place and accurate to within 0.5% of ethanol at 20°C and can be:

1. Labelled wine if it has an alcohol content of between 6.5% and 15% ethanol by volume at 20°C

2. Called a low alcohol beverage if it has no more than 1.15% ethanol by volume at 20°C

3. Called a reduced alcohol wine if it has more than 1.15% but not more than 6.5% of ethanol by volume at 20°C

4. Not represented as de-alcoholised wine unless is contains at most 0.5% of ethanol by volume at 20°C and the grape variety can replace the word wine

5. Called a fortified wine (which is not a prescribed name unlike Port) if it has more that 15% and less than 22% of ethanol by volume at 20°C

These definitions vary around the world. And it may not be just for health or marketing purposes that the alcohol content is listed. A higher alcohol wine attracts higher taxes in many parts of the world.

You may see the words 'proof' on some labels. Proof is simply the percentage of alcohol times 2. If a wine is 14% alcohol it is 28 proof. This is mostly used on spirits rather than wines.

And although this is completely unrelated to winemaking, I found this while researching yeasts years ago and I just like this sort of thing.

Bread flavour is formed in the crust as it reaches a temperature of 150°C to 180°C while the internal bread temperature does not exceed 99°C. The higher temperature causes the sugar in the dough to caramelise creating a fruity or winy odour. Removal of the crust soon after baking prevents the crumb from absorbing the crust flavour causing it to taste different.

Fermenting
The ferment happens some time after we've added the yeast.

Yes, the grape has a natural yeast on the skin. If we crushed our grape and left it in a warm environment it'll start to ferment on its own. However, with these natural yeasts we have no idea what we'll get. What flavours, alcohol, colour extraction, fruit nose, slow ferment, fast ferment, hot ferment, what??? Our hard-earned grape is at the mercy of unknown yeasts and that's just too much risk when you're making premium wines.

That's why we want to kill off the natural yeasts and then inoculate the must with our preferred yeast.

We kill off the natural yeast with a dose of SMS or PMS. That's Sodium Metabisulphite or Potassium Metabisulphite sprinkled in as a powder during crushing. Fortunately the natural yeasts are weak compared to the commercial yeasts.

Then we add in our preferred yeast. Yeast technology has come leaps and bounds in the last ten years. Our first ferments had us starting the yeast in warm water and grape juice. Then we'd slowly add more grape juice until we had a big bucketful of warm, yeasty smelling, frothing, bubbling soup ready to go. We'd gently pour this soup into the tank and then nervously check every few hours to see if the ferment had taken. We'd wander up to the winery every few hours all rugged up to feel and stick our ears to the tanks.

A warm noisy tank means your ferment if off and running.

A cold quiet tank means it's time to brew a fresh yeast soup and spend another few hours in the winery until we could crawl back to our nice warm beds.

To get a 'stuck' ferment going we'd add yeast food (DAP) to the next yeast 'soup' and try again. During the colder vintages we wrapped electric blankets and insulation round the tanks to keep the ferment going. During the warmer vintages we'd move the tanks to the cool rooms to slow down the ferment and avoid the nasty flavours released during hot and quick ferments. We wanted the long slow ferments to release the full fruit flavours and gentle tannins. Not the hot, short, sharp ferments, that's not what we wanted.

With the reds we learnt early on not to overfill the tanks, as the cap overflows the tank. We were hands-on and manual all the way and didn't have the fancy rotary fermenters to keep the cap wet. We did it the manual way by plunging the cap every few hours. It meant that last thing at night and first thing in the morning you'd head up to the winery, get the stick out and push the cap down on each and every tank.

The merlots and pinots were nice and soft and it was an easy job. If you left the shiraz and cab sav overnight then you'd just about walk on the cap by morning. They formed a hard, thick layer wanting constant TLC to stay wet.

With the whites, the most important thing was to keep the temperatures low to preserve the delicate flavours. Even then you'd get times when the ferment went hyperactive and there'd be mess to clean up the next day.

This probably sounds haphazard and all over the shop. Cold vintages, warm vintages, too hot, too cold, too slow or too fast.

But that's what it was like. Every vintage was different, every harvest was different and every year was different.

After the first few vintages I realised the idea of the farmer at one with nature was utter crap. It seemed like an out and out war with nature on one side and me on the other. When you wanted a still dry day to spray some weeds or vines, it'd be blowing a gale. When I desperately hoped and prayed for low humidity and dry days to make the mildews and moulds go away, nature kept sending rain and heat.

When it was so dry the trees were hoping more dogs would stop by, nature simply kept on delivering more dry.

But my attitude changed over the years. And that change was called patience.

Some people learn it by having children, some learn it the hard way and some never learn it.

If nature decides it's going to rain then no amount of screaming, ranting, threatening, pleading, cajoling or begging will change nature's mind. You can throw yourself against nature till you're black and blue all over but that rain will still come down where and when nature wants it to.

Or you can accept nature and go on with something else on your to-do list.

I had the tremendous fortune and privilege of learning patience in nature's open air and rolling hills classroom. And I believe there's no finer classroom in this world than Mother Nature's outdoors for any lesson worth learning.

20 PRESSING GRAPES

The Press

While the winery was still very small we used manual, hand ratchet basket presses. My experience was that they were utter rubbish.

I know the principle has been around for a very, very long time.

I know they're cheap to buy.

I know they're traditional.

However...

They leak, they're slow to load, slow to use and slow to unload. They're a hassle to get the timber blocks right and they're a nightmare to clean.

We stuck with them for the first few seasons and then looked around for something better. We stuck with them because we thought they were the best available since everyone used them and that's the way things were done in the wine industry. Little did we know everyone used them because they were too complacent to look past their local suppliers and experiment and see what the rest of the world had to offer.

Airbag presses were becoming all the rage but a few things put us off like;

The $40,000 price tag.

The stories filtering through about long pressing cycles with no manual override.

The long drawn out cleaning process.

And the final straw was the fragile electronics we kept hearing about.

People were producing monster size hydraulic basket presses but our experiences with the basket press principle left us cold to that approach. All the basket press design flaws still applied to these monsters, it was the same crap design done on a larger crap scale. The only consolation was fewer crap pressing cycles since they fitted more fruit in each crap pressing. The cleaning, the shit flying everywhere, the loading, the unloading, all these 'features' were still there.

The end result was we went low tech and bought a Howard Rotapress. It was secondhand from a winery up country and it was solid, it worked and we've never regretted it for a minute.

We bought a generator as the Rotapress was 3-phase powered and the winery had no 3-phase power.

It was easy to load, produced wonderful results and was easy to unload.

When you let it run the full hi-lo cycle the pressings came out dry and with all seeds intact. You'd pick them up, crush them in your hand and your hand stayed dry.

It was noisy, it moaned and it groaned. It let you know when it wanted more grease by squealing like a baby piglet.

It was a breeze to clean and unload.

It was built like a tank. The German stainless steel was real stainless steel, not the flimsy pretend stainless we got on some tanks. We moved it around with the forklift or three strong guys could wheel it around and for a smallish winery it was an ideal fit.

And in the end Peter K rewired it so we controlled it via a USB interface off a laptop. Not a bad step forward for an ageing electro-mechanical masterpiece.

It was a great investment. It took work to keep running, it cost us some dollars in repairs along the way, it helped produce some great wines and it's still running.

And, like all good agricultural equipment that's reached the end of its life, the basket presses are now garden ornaments and as I've said before, that's the best place for them.

Bunch Press Whites

Most vintages we hand picked the whites to get the best possible quality. And no, I'm not going back on my comments about machine picking giving the same quality as hand picking. When we wanted to bunch press whites, you had no choice. The machine harvest gave us berries and not bunches. So, as you saw in the picking section, we'd first load the fruit into white foam boxes.

When the fruit came into the winery we'd stack it onto pallets, chill it in the cool room overnight and process the next day. This gave us nice low fruit temperatures to cut down oxidisation and it was a breeze to load into the press with convenient, easy to lift, people-friendly sized foam boxes.

It didn't get much easier than this.

Red Must

Loading the press with the reds was a different story. For the whites we're pressing fresh fruit to give us grape juice that we settle and then ferment. With the reds we're pressing the fermented wine. So you've got seeds, pulped skins, alcohol fumes and it's still bubbling.

We sucked up most of the fermented must with a must pump or dumped it straight from the tank, except for the thick shiraz ferments where no pump could pick up the last two feet from the bottom so it was all loaded by bucket and shovel. And I'm not picking on shiraz. It's a wonderful grape to work with and it's a total bastard at the same time. It's a text book love-hate relationship. The vine's hard to work with but it gives you magnificent fruit. The wines need lots of care to give their best but when you get the best, it is truly magnificent. No other grape makes you work so hard but, then again, no other grape rewards you so richly.

And the carbon dioxide settled at the bottom of the tank so you got a headache after about 10 minutes working in there.

It was dirty, it was hard work, but the smell of the ferment was amazing and I sorely miss that.

Walking into the winery first thing in the morning, the heady, rich, fruit, yeasty smell smacks all the senses. No description I can give does justice to this feeling, this smell, this experience, call it what you will.

For the true wine lover there is nothing in the world like this smell.

If you're into your wines then please find some way to get this experience. I promise you the smell will stay with you for this lifetime.

Unloading the Press

Unloading the Rotapress was a snack. We'd pull the wine tray out from underneath, move the press outside and set it running backwards. The pressings fell out, we'd shovel them into the trailer and spread them out on the gardens. The Rotapress design was brilliant in its simplicity.

The native birds loved the grape seeds in the pressings. You'd see dozens of them feeding away, making their bird noises, cracking away at the seeds and having a good feed. The tourists loved this wonderful photo opportunity to see dozens of colourful rosellas, parakeets, etc right in front of them, out in the wild so to speak.

The red grape pressings were (since they're post ferment) quite acid and the native plants loved this. The green grape pressings (pre ferment) are pretty neutral pH wise and worked well anywhere in the gardens. You picked where you put which pressings so the gardens thrived.

It comes back to the attention to detail. We could have dumped the pressing in the paddocks... But, by taking a little extra time we solved a trash disposal problem, created a new tourist attraction and kept the native birds happy.

That's a win-win all round.

And, the kangaroos ate the pressings as well. So now you can rest easily in this lifetime that someone in this world can show you a photo of what kangaroo poo looks like complete with grape seeds. Ain't nature a wonderful thing.

Pressed Wine

The green grape juice coming out of the press is murky and muddy and sickly sweet. It's the same flavour you get from supermarket grape juice but much sweeter and much, much dirtier. The air smells like one giant fruity drink and everything you touch is sticky. The next step is to settle and stabilise it before the ferment.

Pressed red wine comes out murky and muddy with a brilliant bright burgundy purple colour. It tastes rough and ready and unpolished with a strong sharp carbon dioxide bite and fruit nose. From the press it goes into stainless steel tanks to settle or oak to finish the fermentation.

21 MAKING IT ALL WORK TOGETHER

To finish off here's some final words on the disparate parts that make it all work...

No particular order and no particular importance and no particular timings.

Cellar Door Changes

The cellar door started as one tiny little room off the side on the big shed.

As more and more people started exploring wineries and we marketed more we got busier.

The big shed was just that – a big shed. When we first moved in it was a roof and open on two sides. Now this was great as you had breathtaking views but the practically was hovering damn close to zero. It worked like a wind tunnel and sauna all in one.

Keeping it clean was a no-win option as the next breeze brought leaves, grass clippings and whatever else it chose with it. So we made the plans and started to close it in.

This was easier said than done as it took some 2 years to close it up, get the concrete slab poured and put up the toilets. All this was done with council permits that took their own sweet time arriving. But the most amazing part of all this was the final approval from the council building inspector.

He arrived late one wet Friday afternoon and the entire 'inspection' lasted less than 2 minutes. He had a quick glance at the walls, stuck his head in the toilet door and then started filling in the paperwork. To this day I have no idea if he was happy with what he saw and noticed that it was all done 100% correctly or if he just wanted to finish up for the week. And quite frankly I really didn't care as I had my certificate and could open up the next phase of our winery.

We then expanded out to take up half the big shed, as we called it. And not long later on we expanded out to take over all the big shed.

We kept it as it was for a lot of years but started getting more and more functions. A tin shed was fine for a while but we had to lift our game a little and that's when the multitude of windows and doors and glass arrived. It was still a long way away from the sterile glass and architect-gone-wild-with-a-blank-cheque structures you see at some wineries, it still had character and trees and views.

And no matter what we did, people still loved it.

Irrigation

The winery was about as far south as you can get on mainland Australia without getting your feet wet. Just above 1,000mm per year was the average rainfall. And we were on sandy, well-drained soil.

After talking to many people and scouring countless viticultural research papers we planned and implemented a drought proof strategy. We had the perfect subsoil structure to make this work. Most soils have a topsoil layer, a clay layer and then either more clay or rock or whatever as you go down. Most plant life happens in the top 18" (450mm) of soil but there's a vast amount of moisture locked up further down.

Geologically the winery sat on the Health Hill fault line. This fault line pushed up the ridges we planted on and gave us our vast sandy subsoil structure. We had no clay so the vines' roots were free to travel as deep into the earth as they pleased. The only trick was to get the vine to push roots down and not out horizontally in the search for water.

Plant roots travel seeking water. That's why you see shallow roots fanning out from the trunk searching for precious water in the top few inches of soil. Sure, some plants have a deep tap root, but grapevines have fibrous shallow surface roots spreading out horizontally, not a deep tap root.

We installed drip irrigation and used a very low volume single dripper on each vine, around 2 litres (approx 0.5 US gallons) an hour. This low application rate, along with the sandy soil, meant the water soaked into the soil directly under the vine and didn't spread out along the surface. So we trained the vine roots to chase the water deep and not on the surface.

The new plantings needed water and they got it and usually got it every hot summer day. By about year 7 the vines were virtually drought-proof. By virtually, I mean they got 2-4 irrigations during the season and only then when it was very, very dry. The older vines, planted in 1982, haven't seen irrigation for many years and they've produced their best vintages during our droughts.

For us, with the soil we had and with the rainfall we had, this strategy worked stonkingly well.

Now for the mechanics of making it work.

We were fortunate the property was ideal for a gravity fed irrigation setup. We worked off a large concrete water tank at the highest point of the property. It was fed from two dams, one about 1.2km (approx 1,300 yards) away and the other one about 600m away. We used 50mm (2") poly pipe for all the feeds and mains; from there we used 13mm poly and low rate drippers on the in-row feeds.

We re-dug the dams when it became clear we'd need more water. We also found there are some pretty big excavators and bulldozers in use around country Victoria. You stand next to it and look up at the tracks...

I won't gloss over this: it was a lot of work to put this in place.

First we dug the mains. Some we did by trencher and others I did with a pipe layer on the back of a tractor. The pipe layer was much quicker but I couldn't use it everywhere as it just didn't fit.

The 50mm poly pipe comes in 100m rolls. They're about 2m in diameter and the trick was to unroll them without kinking the pipe. It took me over an hour to unroll each roll without the kinks. Then I dragged it with the quad bike so it was close to the fresh dug trenches, joined the pieces together and buried them. It all sounds so simple and elegant when I'm writing this but it was many days of work to get to this stage.

Next we had to get the irrigation lines into the rows. This meant a new wire, 200mm off the ground on the uphill side of the vine. Next was to unroll the 300m long 13mm poly pipe rolls, again without kinking them.

The pros have their racks and spinners to load the roll and peel off as much or as little as needed. We had bare paddock so you work with what you've got.

Once I've got my 13mm pipe laid out straight I have to drag it down the row, anchor it at the far end and then clip it onto the wire at approx 1,200mm intervals which is a **lot** of clips.

Next, a dripper goes on next to each vine. This meant punching a hole in the pipe next to each vine and pushing in the dripper. Every 100m row has approx 45 vines and every block has some 25 rows, so that's approx 1,125 vines which translates to a lot of time spent on your knees pushing in drippers. And there's the times you punch straight through the pipe and need a 'goof' plug on the other side to fix what you just stuffed.

Finally we connect the 13mm pipe back into the mains. This means drilling a hole in the main, jamming in a grommet, sticking in the barb fitting and pushing through the 13mm pipe. Provided you don't push the drill through to the other side of the pipe and then have to repair that before you can get back to what you were originally doing.

All up, it was a lot of work on your hands and knees and leaning down into the trench.

We used a 300 micron filter going into the tank and then another 300 micron filter before it fed out to each block. We bought 'take-apart' drippers so it was easy to clean any blocked ones. Later on we bought the non-take-apart drippers as they just didn't get blocked. Ever.

From the main water tank we went to a 'distribution block' of simple 50mm ball valves to send water to each block.

It was low tech and low power and you had to constantly check and it begged for continuous maintenance.

It was simple, it was manual and it worked.

But it was still physical hard work to make it happen. The first irrigation of any season was the worst. Without fail, we'd torn up some section of irrigation during each off-season so it was out there with the shovel, joiners and spares patching it all back together. And then you'd cruise up and down each row checking each individual dripper. I found the quickest way to find the dud drippers was by sound. Your senses key into the environment around you and for me the sound, or more specifically the lack of sound, coming from a dud dripper was my trigger for the next 'stop and fix'. This went pretty quickly but it was still a task we had to do each season, in fact each time we irrigated. The kangaroos would be fighting in the vines and pull apart a drip line with their tails or you'd catch one with the mower. Just something. Always there was some damage we'd do in the process.

So it was more work on top of the rest of the tasks and it was invariably hot and sticky when I was digging or patching or joining or fixing pumps. It was hard work and it was hot work and usually muddy work to boot.

But when you saw all the drippers running in the last light of the day it was pure magic. The scene was magnificent and the light dancing off the forest of droplets was mesmerising.

The smell was something that you never ever get in the city. The earth's taking a drink after a long thirst and there's no smell in the world like it. The warm, moist, rich earthy smell wafting up was pure bliss for the soul and one of the memories that'll stay with me till my last breath in this life.

Sign at the Front

Hopefully you've noticed by now that we liked 'big' projects.

We ummed and ahhhed about the sign at the front gate for quite a while. Perhaps two traditional sandstone walls flanking the entrance with the winery name arrogantly branded on each side?

Maybe a wine barrel on a pedestal or a stylised grapevine?

Eventually the big wine bottle and glass shape sign won out – about 10m tall is what we mean by big. All of this was made on the property, by hand, from locally rolled parts.

First we cut and welded it together in the shape of a bottle and wine glass. I did the wine bottle a little too much in the shape of a beer bottle but none of the thousands of people who've seen it, photographed it and touched it have complained. It was days of work to cut, weld and paint this. We welded on some reinforcing mesh normally used in concrete and give us something to put other signs onto.

Then we made up the vinyl sign for "The Gurdies Winery". We had the vinyl cutter, so while this took many hours to design and cut, we got exactly what we wanted. (see the Signs section for more details on the cutter). The sign has the same blue and white reflective vinyl used on street signs so driving up the road you can see it for miles.

Physically putting the sign up was the easiest part. With help from the neighbours it was up and concreted down and bolted together in a few hours.

Now it's a local landmark and reference point.

Signs

A key tool for the engraved bottles work was the vinyl cutter. After we'd been working on the bottles for a while it dawned on us that we could use the cutter for what it was originally intended, that is to make signs.

To buy professional made banners and signs was out of our budget, but we could buy the raw materials and make our own for a fraction of the price.

Our first efforts were truly woeful. The design was shocking, the colour combinations would make a blind man blush and they were unreadable on the road side. But, after studying every design handbook and sign making magazine I could lay my hands on - we got better.

The signs worked and they worked well. I cover the wine and cheese days in a separate section but the roadside signs we put out for our festivals successfully pulled many people off the main road and into our winery.

Naturally that was once we got our sizes and designs right. The two key concepts I found from our sign making days were that:

1) The word "free" works to get attention and pull in people
2) Your design must communicate the message in 8 seconds or less to someone driving past at 100kph

Vinyl cut signs account for about 95% of all signs you see around you. The process involves computer cutting the letter or design outline and then weeding, or painstakingly hand picking, the background vinyl away from the parts we want to keep. Then we stick on a transfer tape to transfer the sign lettering onto the sign.

It's another operation that rolls off the tongue so easily…

One paragraph above covered hundreds of hours of learning time and perfecting time and getting the nuances right.

It's the weeding part that takes a very long time. We'd sit there with an Exacto knife night after night, weeding out the backgrounds. Then the operation to transfer the letters to the background started. It was real easy to get it wrong at this stage, as once you've got the transfer tape on and the vinyl off the backing, the vinyl turns into a massive sheet of flypaper that actively seeks out any surface within reach other than the one you're aiming for.

The Easter Harvest Festival measured 4m by 6m so it's not small. The bunny rabbit is cut from two strips of vinyl and joined on the sign. The lettering is cut in strips and lined up on the sign.

The "live band" one is 6m x 1m. It's big enough to see clearly at highway speeds and it's simple enough to directly communicate the message. And it worked.

The smaller signs we had under the "St Helier Road Wineries" road signs worked a treat.

About 25% of our festival traffic came from these signs and even more for our 'wine and cheese' days.

Anyway, the signs worked and we got the passing trade that we would otherwise have missed. For us, the return on investment was worth it even though making them took many, many hours of effort and drove us clean up the wall.

Aerial View

We wanted to see the property layout from the air. So we hired a light plane and went for a flight.

Our pilot had obviously done this before and all I had to do was point him towards the winery. We popped open a side window and while he circled around I snapped away like crazy.

We took piccies of the other wineries in St Helier Road and our neighbours and gave them all copies. They were a little puzzled why we'd do this but said thanks anyway.

What floored me was how my perspective of the property layout changed. Vine blocks I thought were square onto each other appeared skew-whiff. And fences I thought were a long way off were quite close by.

It changed my view of the property and the area as well.

Cutting Timber Slabs

The water views came at a price. We got the ferocious storms and winds pretty much straight out of Antarctica. Tasmania to the south was a mere speed bump.

Each storm brought fresh challenges and frustrations. One blew off the bird netting and every spring storm bashed the precious shoots and flowers. Winter storms kept us inside when we should have been out pruning and the consistent winds made regular sprays a challenge. But, the views were breathtaking.

The bigger storms took their toll on the trees. Every blow brought down fresh branches so firewood was never a problem. After we lost some big trees we decided to use the trunks as tabletops.

First of all we had to 'slab' them. That's timber-cutting talk for cutting them along the grain into table sized slabs.

The guy doing the slabbing arrived with his trusty Lucas Mill and set up around the first trunk. Some 45 minutes later we were cutting our first slab.

The Lucas Mill is a super size chain saw turned side on. You set up the frame, load the monster chainsaw and push it through the log to make each cut.

By the time we'd cut some 8 slabs there was a mountain of sawdust and a stack of good looking table tops. All up we cut close to 30 slabs and ended up with lots of stunning, individual tables.

We were lucky as the tree trunks had naturally air dried over the years so we didn't have to kiln dry them, all we had to do was to slab them. This saved a lot of time and expense. Some of them have cracked over the years and this has only added to the character.

Timber Slab Tables

We used old Singer treadle sewing machine bases as our table legs. I'm sure we cleaned out every antique store in a 500km radius to get these legs. Some were newer, some were older, some were copies while some were originals. And they all found a home under our tabletops.

We used a clear lacquer to highlight the natural grain and flaws. This worked really well and lasted through lots of wear, tear and abuse.

The outside ones are starting to show their age now and somehow that simply adds to the character.

It was a LOT of work to sand them, clean them up, finish them and get them into the winery.

And the end result was worth it. Most people would walk up to the tables and start running their hands over them. The guys would bend over the have a look underneath to see how the legs were attached. Everybody had something to say about them.

BBQ Area

The BBQ area grew from a small concrete slab to a galvanised steel undercover outbuilding.

We started with a flat, level concrete slab and here's an example of Murphy's Law at its finest.

I laid kilometres and kilometres of irrigation lines around the winery. Most were under the vines but a lot were in the gardens to fight off the long dry summers. Most were 50mm poly pipes but some were 25mm poly pipes. And a 25mm poly pipe is pretty small. Put two fingers together and you'll get the idea about how thick a 25mm poly pipe really is. When you're digging around trying to find it, it's something pretty easy to miss and really, really hard to find.

Now...

When I was putting in the formwork for the slab I hit a 25mm poly pipe with the formwork pegs 4 times.

FOUR: one, two, three, four.

Four times I hit one stupid little pipe. So a half day exercise to do some formwork turned into a full day dig-a-thon to fix what I'd just destroyed. And that meant another drive to the hardware supply store to get the parts to fix it. I always kept some spares but not 4 of each thing.

There really were times when I'd look around trying to find the 'candid camera' crew as reality couldn't possibly be as strange as what was happening to me.

After the basic flat concrete slab came the sails.

This was around 2003 when sails and stainless steel wires were all the rage. The nautical look was in and it didn't matter if you got seasick in the bathtub, you had to have 'the look'.

The main vertical supports were simply tree trunks cut off the property. Little did I realise this was to be our undoing, but that's later on in the story.

I got a guy with a Dingo digger (mini excavator-like digger in Australia) to drill the holes in the ground as there was just no way in the world I was going to dig 4 feet of summer baked clay by hand. And then we got a crane truck in to lift the poles into the holes. So far so good and in a few short hours my poles were standing upright and pointing every which way except where I wanted them to.

And as is usually the case when planning is enhanced with a few glasses of red, what seems really simple rapidly turns into a multi-day task when you're actually doing it. I spent the next days with a hand winch, a tractor and every rope, strap and chain we had lining up the poles and concreting them in.

So far so good it seemed.

Putting up the sails themselves was pretty easy. I used chains and turnbuckles to line them up how I wanted. They looked absolutely fantastic when done and we got plenty of comments and photos. And they lasted a fair few years.

However, we got howling winds regularly and it was only a matter of time before something gave way. One of the tree trunks I'd used was less than solid and snapped during a gale. The chain was still attached to the sail and this managed to shred the sail while flapping around in the gale.

So down came the sails and we went onto plan B. This was a steel and corrugated iron shelter that even the big bad wolf could never blow down.

In the end I cut off the timber poles at ground level and that was the last evidence of the sails gone forever.

The steel version survived many gales, floods, scorching summers and freezing winters and it's still standing. There have been countless BBQs, weddings, functions, picnics, you name it in that shelter and it's still there.

I guess I can call that a success story.

The Driveways

While we're talking about impressions, the driveways and parking areas took a surprising amount of maintenance. The summers were OK but the wet winters really pounded the driveways. The heavy coach and bus traffic churned up the drive like no ones business during the wet times.

I was out with the tractor grading the driveways what seemed like every few weeks and while that doesn't sound like a lot of work it's still something that has to be done. It's another task that comes up on you and it's another task that takes time.

You know yourself, when you visit somewhere with potholes in the driveway, your first impression takes a nosedive.

We rebuilt the driveway several times. Sometimes it was as simple as a dozen truck loads of gravel and a grader. Other times it was full on roadworks with the excavators, graders and many, many truck loads of fill. And even then the potholes come back after a few months.

It's another unseen cost to most people. They drive in to your place, they expect clean easy access and that's fair enough. You're there to sell yourself and every little bit helps and the first impression is so very important and YOUR attention to detail makes this happen. It's up to YOU to keep the place clean and looking fantastic.

My customers saw a nice, well maintained, graded driveway.

I saw a $35,000 invoice…

The Gardens

The gardens took a lot of time to setup and a lot of time to maintain.

If you don't like gardening or can't pay a gardener then it's a struggle.

It comes back to people judging you the moment they set foot on the place. When the lawns were mowed and the place looked a treat, we sold more wines. When the lawns weren't fresh cut (and that can mean twice a week in spring) people tended to buy less.

We started with a blank paddock. The garden beds, the flowers, the trees, they don't all happen overnight.

We brought in tons and tons and tons of top soils and mulch to get the gardens established. We lost a lot of expensive plants until we decided to stick with Australian, drought resistant native plants. Now the gardens look fantastic all year round and we didn't lose any plants even during the drought years.

We found the key to a great garden was to imagine what the place will look like in five years time.

For some people, that's easy. For others it'd be easier to sprout wings and fly.

Some of the plants ended up too close together and we ripped some out and moved others. Some died during the move. But you have to keep going and going and work with the end goal in mind.

A winery is not a 'get rich quick' scheme. It's an investment and it's a long term investment.

Just remember, there is a lot of work to keep the place looking customer friendly.

Sheds

At every paragraph I've resisted waxing on about what we should have done and carrying on about the benefit of hindsight and generally crapping on like an old fart who's done it all.

I'll break that resolution here for one single sentence. Here it is.

If I had the chance to do all this again, I wouldn't add on sheds to sheds as we went along, I'd put down an acre of concrete and build one monster shed on it.

There, the preaching's done.

We started with a bare shed open on two sides while one small shed served as tasting room and dry storage. A tiny little 'cut off' served as tool room and a bit of 'lock up' space for the few tools we had.

And we had an old railway carriage on the property as well. The original owners lived in this while they built the main house. It would have been wonderful to convert it into a cellar door but it had been neglected for way too long. If you touched one thing, something next to it fell down in sympathy. In the end we gave up and a couple from country Mildura (300km away) bought it. They trucked it up there and turned it into a B&B so at least it went to a good home.

Soon the open sides were closed over and the tasting 'room' turned into the tasting 'half shed'.

Not too much later the tasting 'half shed' turned into the tasting building complete with 20 metre bar. And finally after much more concrete and walls and windows it ended up a place where people walked in and said; 'Wow'.

It was a nice way to finish off. And it was nice for other people to appreciate and enjoy the building where we'd poured in our work, time, sweat and money.

A new machinery shed sprouted while the old one morphed into a cool room. Yet more concrete made the new machinery shed forklift-friendly so moving pallet loads out of storage was a breeze.

By this stage I was on a first name basis with our concrete suppliers. We poured most of the concrete ourselves as time and resources permitted. At one stage it rained for about eight or nine of our 'pours' in a row. The concrete supplier would start laughing as soon as he heard my voice on the phone. I didn't even have to say what we wanted, he'd just start laughing and joking about how he's glad I'm calling as we needed the rain. Anyway, I'm glad we helped the district with our rainmaking efforts.

As for the conifers now towering over the sheds, the plant identification tag for these trees read 3-4m in height when fully grown. Now that they're twice that height it's a little hard complaining to the nursery about their inaccurate labels.

At no time while we were building our modest winery did we ever dream we'd have so many sheds or such a beautiful tasting room. All that seemed so far away and so unachievable. But with a consistent and determined effort we achieved it all. There were many setbacks; there were floods when it rained, strong winds blew in my sliding doors, air conditioners failed at the worst possible times, heavy rain on the unlined tin roof sounded like a jumbo jet at takeoff and we changed the layout more times than a politician's promises.

But we did it.

With time and a vision we did it.

Tractors

We ran all our implements from two Farmliner 45 horsepower tractors. Farmliner was a Romanian made copy of an old FIAT design. That now seems a laughable situation but that's what we had so that's what we used.

They were primitive, they were low-tech and they were slow. On the upside, they'd run all day on half a tank of fuel and with such low horsepower we didn't break much equipment and regular maintenance costs were trivial compared to the high-tech marvels in vine rows across the country.

The only major repairs were a new clutch to the 2WD and a new motor to the 4WD one. How the staff managed to put a con rod (major engine part that usually breaks in high-performance sports cars, not tractors) through the side of the block on a low horsepower, low revving diesel is beyond me to this day. But destroy it they did.

The 2WD had a very hard life and every panel was damaged in some way. Most of the instruments had broken and I was simply too busy to keep up the maintenance but they chugged along despite the lack of tender loving care.

We didn't do massive hours on the machinery; they both had less than 4,000 hours in close to 20 years which by farming standards is nothing. And the tyre wear was minimal as both tractors still had their original tyres. We simply did not wear them out.

What I missed most was a cab on at least one of the tractors. The open ROPS layout gave perfect all round vision, but you fried in summer, had a wet arse in winter and had to wear a space suit while spraying.

We made all sorts for frames and jigs to do particular tasks. Some worked a treat, some were unmitigated disasters, but we got the job done.

ABOUT THE AUTHOR

When I talk to people about what we've done the first thing they say is; 'Wow, we've always wanted to own a winery'. And after we go through that conversation the next question without fail is; 'Would you do it again?'
The answer is unequivocally; yes.
We had some tough times and we had some lean years but the experiences I've got and the end result made every minute of it worthwhile.
I've made lifelong friends who I know will be with me till the day they're screwing down the lid. And to be fair, I've also lost friends who I now see were there only for the good times.
I've learnt a brain snapping amount about people, nature and everything else under the sun. And the things I now know you can achieve when you set your mind to it have stretched me way beyond the person I was when we started this venture.
And I also know in the dark of night when I'm drifting off to sleep that I've crossed one major thing off my bucket list;
I've had the privilege of being one of the relative handful of people in this world to make wine in my own winery with grapes from my own vineyard.
Remember life is short and always live your dreams…

Peter Svans

Connect with Me online
www.thisdayinwine.com
Twitter: #thisdayinwine
Facebook: thisdayinwine
Instagram: thisdayinwine
Pinterest: thisdayinwine

64779954R00108

Made in the USA
Middletown, DE
17 February 2018